ADVERTISING TODAY AND TOMORROW

UNWIN PROFESSIONAL MANAGEMENT LIBRARY

Company Organization: Theory and Practice
PA Management Consultants Limited
M. C. Barnes, A. H. Fogg, C. N. Stephens, L. G. Titman

Marketing and Higher Management
PA Management Consultants Limited
Esmond Pearce

Effective Industrial Selling
Vic Markham

Planning the Corporate Reputation
Vic Markham

Managing the Training Function
Christopher Gane

Managing for Profit – The Added Value Concept
R. R. Gilchrist

The Organization Gap
R. B. Kemball-Cook

Computers, Management and Information
David Firnberg

Decisions, Strategies and New Ventures
W. G. Byrnes and B. K. Chesterton

Systems Analysis in Business
John Graham

The Multinational Man
Thomas Aitken

ADVERTISING TODAY AND TOMORROW

W. A. EVANS

Lecturer in Marketing, Cranfield School of Management

London

GEORGE ALLEN & UNWIN LTD

RUSKIN HOUSE MUSEUM STREET

First published in 1974

ISBN 0 04 658210 x

Printed in Great Britain
in Times 327 11 on 13
by The Aldine Press, Letchworth

Acknowledgements

Any discussion of advertising owes much to example, and I am indebted to the following companies for permission to reproduce material: Bovril Group Marketing Ltd, Cadbury Schweppes Ltd, the Gillette Company, Arthur Guinness, Son, & Co. Ltd, Hobson Bates & Partners Ltd, Peter Kenny, Unilever Ltd and A. Wander Ltd.

I also wish to thank the following for permission to quote from published writings: Dr R. H. Beck, F. H. K. Henrion, John Hobson, Philip Kotler, David Ogilvy, Rosser Reeves, Carl F. Braun and Leslie Rodger.

During the preparation of this book I have been encouraged and stimulated by conversation with my faculty colleagues and my students at the Business School, but I hasten to add that the responsibility for the views expressed is entirely my own. My family, too, deserves thanks for its patience and forbearance, as does The Swan at Fressingfield for inspiration when the Muse failed.

Finally, I must acknowledge my gratitude to Audrey Bond and Dot Martin for cheerfully and accurately typing my manuscript.

Preface

There has been at the same time both too much and too little written about advertising.

On the one hand, the personal memoirs of some of the more successful practitioners, often sensational and almost inevitably the result of a desire to promote the interests of their own companies, have produced a bibliography of the business which, though much more interesting, is of only slightly higher value than the ghosted reminiscences of pre-eminent idols of sport. In attempting to propound what are euphemistically referred to as advertising philosophies, such men have succeeded, unwittingly, in writing what can only be described as a sort of non-fiction version of *The Carpetbaggers*.

This is no fault of theirs, of course. As practising advertising men they were perhaps far too centrally concerned with the problems of winning and keeping business (and there is no doubt that both Rosser Reeves and David Ogilvy, to quote but two, gained a lot of new clients through their books); they were too much on the inside and not sufficiently committed to the functions and responsibilities of advertising as only one of many pieces in a much greater puzzle, the puzzle of industrial activity, of planning, producing and promoting products.

Advertising people, for all their protests to the contrary, tend to be a very inbred bunch; clever, yes, but frequently divorced from the realities of business life. The result is that whenever one of them writes a book this rarefied atmosphere shows through and their readers go away with the feeling that it is all rather a game. Advertising is its own worst enemy and its own worst advocate, which is an appalling paradox.

On the other hand, most people who write about advertising from the outside (observing it either as a business function or a social phenomenon) fail to do it justice because, while they may be able to describe its structure and its purpose, they are usually incapable of touching the fire in its belly. Thus you will find creativity, the driving force of advertising, reduced to an academic treatise by the serious literature of the business, and you will find the odd chapter about advertising in a book on marketing which sounds very nervous because at that point the author finds himself short of formulas and has to start talking about an art and not a science.

Both these types of literature, therefore, fail in their own way, the one through self-centredness and removal from reality, the other through lack of understanding. *Advertising is a highly professional activity* (I choose the word 'professional' with some care, since anyone who takes the trouble to read this book will realise that it has two meanings in the present context), and it is really only an advertising man who can talk about it and describe what it does with the proper admixture of appreciation and comprehension. What is more, advertising can be discussed meaningfully only through an examination of its central organisations, the many advertising agencies which produce the material to fill newspaper space and television air-time every day. As the business is organised at the moment, advertising *is* advertising agencies.

At the same time, an advertising man who is still actively involved in the business cannot be fully objective about it: he is bound to be influenced by his own environment. This is why I have put five years between myself and my last agency payslip before committing my views to paper; I can now stand back and look at the whole picture without being confused by the details.

I have spent many years of my life in one advertising agency or another. Most of them have been very happy, because advertising has the attraction of being a many-sided and fascinating pursuit. Were I still in the business, I should also feel, out of loyalty perhaps, a little diffident in expressing the attitudes contained in this book since many of them are critical of the industry which paid my salary for so long.

What this book sets out to achieve is to survey the structure and function of modern advertising (and in particular the modern advertising agency), to investigate how appropriate its machinery is for modern business requirements, and to suggest how, both for the good of itself and its clients, it can best equip and refine itself for the future.

The book is, I suppose, a textbook. At least I hope that it will be of some use to students of business, particularly of marketing, in the colleges, universities and business schools. I hope, also, that it will help young people who are seeking to make advertising their career. Most of all, however, I hope it will interest advertising people themselves, for I genuinely believe that the next ten or twenty years are going to see the most significant and far-reaching developments in the structure of the business that it has ever experienced, and that at the end of that time the agency as we know it today may well have disappeared.

I cannot end this preface without recording the debt I owe to my many friends and mentors in the business, too numerous to single out for individual mention. While some, perhaps most, may disagree with the views expressed in this book, they can at least draw comfort from the fact that any criticisms I make are of advertising itself and are, without exception, impersonal.

W.A.E.
Fressingfield, Suffolk

Contents

Illustrations

PART I

Chapter 1

Advertising Yesterday

Personal Communication

If advertising were a profession (which it is not), it would almost certainly by now have been described by somebody as the second oldest profession in the world. If the description has no other merit, it at least serves to indicate how long advertising has been with us, not as an organised industry but as a more personal activity, unnoticed, unintentional, innocuous, indulged in every day by all of us as part of the business of projecting ourselves and our personalities, communicating to others the intricate patterns of our own identities, ideas and idiosyncrasies.

Our motives for self-advertisement vary, of course, a great deal; some are good, some bad. The same is true of the results; indeed, most of the time we advertise ourselves unconsciously, and it is this quality which makes advertising inseparable from our very existence.

It is not, however, on this level that this book will discuss advertising; it is rather on advertising as a tool of mass communication that we shall concentrate – communication seen, heard and experienced every day by everyone through hundreds and thousands of messages in the written and spoken word; and in order to understand the complex structure of modern advertising, shaped and fashioned as it has been by the technological marvels of the twentieth century, we must first trace its growth and development through the ages. For since advertising is so inevitably a part of our social scene, its evolution is part of our social history.

This ubiquitous presence of advertising is deceptive. It might be thought that its very quantity would dull its edge and, like a surfeit of rich food, impair the appetite. Yet much as people may feel that they are ignoring it, frequently they are inadvertently reacting to it; our industrialists are far too profit-conscious to spend the amounts they do on advertising without the expectation of return. The phenomenon is taken so much for granted that few of us pause to think (beyond the occasional passing comment on its humour or its technique, its dullness or its banality) what goes into its creation, why it is happening, or what it is trying to achieve.

Perhaps the reason is that few advertisements are directed at all people. In this modern age of finely differentiated market segments the promotional wavelength is very narrow and target audiences are very precise. Even the same product sold to different prospective customers can require a very different message, like the small motor car which can be offered to readers of the *Daily Mirror* as a prime method of transport and to readers of *The Times* as a shopping runabout. Yet the business of advertising is still an imperfect science, and advertisers must accept that to reach their target markets they will have to tolerate some wastage of readership or viewership. Thus we all see advertisements which are largely irrelevant to our needs, and they pass unnoticed.

Also, the focus of advertising has tended to change with changing conditions of life. These days most advertising concentrates on discretionary purchases, a perfect example of Maslow's hierarchy of needs in practice; in the old days the emphasis was very much on the essentials of existence – staple commodities, patent medicines, basic tools – but these requirements are now largely taken for granted. If you open your morning paper or your magazine, if you watch an evening's television, if you examine the hoardings in the high street, you will find that for the most part they advertise the things you could in theory quite well do without: cosmetics, convenience foods, electric toothbrushes, sweets, exotic drinks, hi-fi, packaged holidays and the rest. These are not absolutely imperative, but they make life more enjoyable, and they are rapidly becoming necessities in an age in which it is difficult to define the meaning of luxury goods; for who is to say that we should not have them?

Were it not for advertising, we should not be as we are: our habits, our attitudes, our possessions, perhaps even our very characters would be in some way different and the world would not be like the world in which we now have our being. Some people claim that it would be a better world; they may be right, but we cannot now change what has happened, and even if organised advertising were to be abolished tomorrow the effects of its past activity would be indelible. They cannot, like an old currency, be withdrawn from circulation and exchanged for something new and different overnight.

History and Development

Early Civilisations. We have to go back to the very beginnings of recorded history to discover the first examples of advertising. On the shards, bricks and tiles unearthed from the buried ruins of early Mediterranean civilisations we find the signatures and imprints of the artists and craftsmen who made them, thus permanently identifying their origin and telling those who saw them where to come back for more. The distinction between an art and a craft was not then a very clear one, nor did it become any clearer for a very long time; this tradition of signing the finished product has continued down the centuries from pre-classical times, through the great sculptures of fifth- and fourth-century Athens, the monuments and household products of imperial Rome, the great cathedrals of the medieval masons and the timber-framed houses of the jobbing builder, to the potters who provide us with our modern breakfast cups and butter dishes. All these things proclaim the identity of their makers, some in pride and some for profit, but they all 'advertise' in the modern sense of the term (first employed by Shakespeare) 'to bring to the notice of'.

Ancient Rome. It is in classical times that we find the first instances of poster advertising, consisting sometimes of commercial publicity for household services but mostly of political propaganda and personal insults. Visitors to Pompeii can see, as clear and as legible as on the day it was written 1,900 years ago, an exhortation daubed on a wall in bold red letters to vote for Furius, who was standing for political office and who, we are informed, was a 'good man'.

In the internecine squabbles which punctuated the last years of the Roman republic, the warring factions (such as the followers of Clodius and Milo, immortalised by Cicero) would conduct their battles not only with the sword but also the pen (or rather the paintbrush), plastering the city buildings with their choicest insults.

Roman trade announcements give us a very clear idea of the types of commerce conducted at the time, but perhaps the most famous of all are the notices advertising forthcoming public entertainments, in particular the gladiatorial combats so dear to the Roman heart and pre-empting by centuries the gay and dramatic billposting of modern Spanish *corridas*.

Ancient Rome supplies us with our first 'commercial break'. M. Porcius Cato, elected censor in 184 B.C., conducted in the Senate his own personal publicity programme for the destruction of Carthage, which, in his opinion, represented a constant threat to the safety of Rome. Whatever the subject under debate, Cato ended every speech he made with the words '*Delenda est Carthago*' (Carthage must be destroyed) before resuming his seat. His campaign was effective: the Romans eventually razed the city to the ground.

The First Printing Process. The practice and purpose of advertising changed very little in the first 1500 years A.D. The reason is not hard to find: no advances were made in the two prime areas which constitute both the possibility and necessity of advertising practice – on the one hand the means of mass communication, on the other the need to employ it. The possibility was provided by the invention of printing, which represented the first major extension of the opportunity to advertise: communication could at last be conducted on the grand scale, the same message could be reproduced hundreds, thousands of times, and its audience could be broadened immeasurably. The new printing process gave rise to the newspaper, first on a local and limited, and then on a national and unlimited scale. As well as newspapers came pamphlets, circulars and posters, leaflets, broadsheets and tracts. The communications industry had been born.

Extension of Horizons. Advertising, then, had at last extended its horizons further than the eye could see. The possibilities had been created, but it was not until the great upheaval in industry at the end of the eighteenth and the beginning of the nineteenth centuries that the necessity to advertise arose on a scale never previously envisaged. The industrial revolution provided the real ingredients of the modern sales and marketing operation: firstly, the production of goods in mass quantity; secondly, the need for mass distribution to enable these goods to be sold; and thirdly, the need for mass communication to promote their qualities and thus facilitate the selling process.

It is really from this time that we begin to measure the growth of the bread-and-butter of advertising – packaged goods – and the emergence of the system which has developed as a result, the advertising agency.

The First Agency. It is a curious fact, and perhaps unique to advertising, that the way in which the modern advertising agency operates is in essence identical to that which was put into practice in the first agency to be created. It is to an American, Volney Palmer, in 1841, that the credit for founding the first agency must go; he was a dealer in real estate, wood, coal and other commodities in Philadelphia, and at the same time he solicited advertising revenue for a number of local newspapers in New Jersey and Pennsylvania. This side of his business developed rapidly: he made it quite clear to his 'clients' that the newspapers were his principals and that he was their 'agent'. His clients were charged no more for their advertising space than if they had bought it direct from the newspaper, and Palmer was paid an agreed commission by the newspapers. He was very successful, and soon had branches in other cities, including New York, Boston and Baltimore, but it is doubtful whether, successful as he was, he ever realised that he had founded a totally new industry, which, by 1973, would be accounting for a turnover of over £600m a year in Great Britain alone.

While Volney Palmer gets the credit as the founding father of modern advertising, he must also be held responsible for its inherent anomalies. These will be discussed in full in a later chapter, but it must be confessed that for an industry to operate for almost a century and a half on business principles which were created virtually by accident is, to say the least, remarkable.

The Golden Age. The nineteenth and early twentieth centuries were, for advertising, the age of the flamboyant and spectacular, as they were for so many other aspects of life. Present-day advertising may be characterised by tricks and gimmicks, but they are nothing to the antics of Barnum and Bailey, Barratt or Carroll, the great sensationalists of the early days. One of the favourite stories amongst advertising men is of the notice erected in Barnum and Bailey's travelling zoo pointing 'To the egress'; movement of customers was consequently brisk to see this intriguing beast, which turned out to be nothing more exciting than the exit.

William Hesketh Lever (the first Lord Leverhulme), in 1891, sent a pavement artist to South Africa to advertise Sunlight Soap, appoint new agents and carry out sampling operations. The artist's name was Carroll and, after an initial setback when he failed to get permission to have 'Sunlight Soap' written on Table Mountain in letters large enough to be read by everyone in the city of Cape Town, he reached Port Elizabeth determined to cause a sensation; rather than risk a second refusal, he acted without asking for permission for what he was doing. Thus it was that two days after Carroll's arrival Port Elizabeth woke up to find the words 'Sunlight Soap' stencilled neatly at regular intervals on both pavements of its main street. Naturally enough, the publicity was immense, and Carroll coolly answered the mayor's anger by promising that, if he had offended any of the city's bye-laws, he would pay for the removal of the signs: 'Mr Mayor, buy a case of Sunlight Soap and set your men to work.' The mayor was mollified, and the signs were scrubbed out – by the very product they advertised.

On a more public-spirited plane, the Boer War provided Bovril with a splendid promotional opportunity. A 'Bovril War Cables' Service was set up, using a fleet of khaki-clad bicyclists to bring important war news to shops in the London area. News of the relief of Ladysmith was wired to the headmasters of schools throughout the country, giving rise in many cases to the award of a half-holiday. The *Sphere*, reporting the incident (14 April 1900), commented drily that 'these boys will certainly grow up with immense faith in the advertiser's art'. (It is, incidentally, to Bovril that the S. H. Benson agency owes its foundation; Benson himself was a Bovril employee until he set up in business on his own account in 1893 with Bovril as his first client.) The advertiser's art was still uncertain and wayward at this time, sometimes brilliant, sometimes banal, sometimes simply shocking; but through the confusion the great figures stand out. Thomas J. Barratt, described by Lord Northcliffe as 'The Father of Modern Advertising', is one such; head of A. & F. Pears, the soap manufacturers, he embarked on an advertising programme on a scale never seen before. In the 1880s he was spending at the rate of £126,000 a year, without an agency. One of his great fancies was testimonial advertising, particularly testimonials from men of medicine and chemistry praising his soap's hygienic qualities; but his most famous testimonial of all was used to promote its beautifying virtues. Pre-empting Lux by several decades, he persuaded the actress Lillie Langtry to claim in an advertisement 'Since using Pears' Soap I have discarded all others'. (*Punch* parodied the advertisement by showing a tramp writing his own version: 'Two years ago I used your soap. Since when I have used no other.' Barratt borrowed the cartoon at once.) The Langtry advertisement had an unfortunate sequel: the actress's signature appeared under her testimonial, and the temptation was too much for one experienced thief – he forged her signature and lifted £40,000 of jewels from her bank, many of them bought with Barratt's money.

It was Barratt also who, when he visited the United States, gatecrashed a reception given by Henry Ward Beecher, the spiritual leader and brother of the author of *Uncle Tom's Cabin*, and persuaded him to write a testimonial for Pears' Soap. Barratt immediately cabled the owner of the *New York Herald*, who was in Paris at the time, and negotiated the unprecedented purchase of the paper's whole front page on which he displayed Beecher's testimonial in full.

Barratt was associated with many of advertising's great events. He took to publishing and introduced *Pears Cyclopaedia*. He also purchased from Sir John Millais the famous painting of 'Bubbles' and much to the artist's consternation (and later delight) reproduced it as a Pears advertisement from a chromo-lithograph. In this he offended Marie Corelli who wrote in 1895:[1]

I am one of those who think the fame of Millais as an artist was marred when he degraded himself to the level of painting the little green boy blowing bubbles of Pears soap. That was an advertisement and that very incident in his career, trifling as it seems, will prevent him ever standing on the dignified height of distinction with such masters in Art as Romney, Sir Peter Lely, Gainsborough and Reynolds.

It is doubtful whether the four august gentlemen she quotes would have shared her horror at Millais's action; certainly Aubrey Beardsley had no hesitation in turning his hand to advertising, for he is on record as saying,

Advertisement is an absolute necessity of modern life, and if it can be made beautiful as well as obvious so much the better for the makers of soap and the public who are likely to wash. . . . the poster first of all justifies its existence on the grounds of utility and should it further aspire

[1] Marie Corelli, *The Sorrows of Satan* (Methuen, 1895).

to beauty of line and colour, may not our hoardings claim kinship with the galleries and the designers of *affiches* pose as proudly in the public eye as the masters of Holland Road or Bond Street Barbizon . . . ? . . . London will soon be resplendent with advertisements. . . . Beauty has laid siege to the city.[1]

In 1880 Barratt imported a quarter of a million French ten-centime pieces and had the name 'Pears' stamped all over them. This caused great consternation in official circles, which culminated in Parliament passing a law declaring all foreign coins to be illegal tender. It is inconceivable that such things should happen today, as it is that Bovril should be as insensitive to the demands of good taste as they were in the 1890s when they ran an advertisement showing a drawing of the Pope holding a mug of Bovril under the headline 'The two infallible powers, THE POPE & BOVRIL'.

There was a sense of novelty, almost of adventure, during these years, and the great figures of advertising tended to be the industrialists themselves rather than the advertising agents. There was also a lack of precision and an extravagance which led Leverhulme to comment wryly that he knew that half of his advertising expenditure was wasted but that he had never been able to discover which half.

Nevertheless, despite his oft-quoted aphorism, Lord Leverhulme also knew that half of his advertising expenditure was *not* wasted, and was determined to go on spending at an ever-increasing weight. It is perhaps one of the most powerful arguments for the effectiveness of advertising to point to the products of those days (at the turn of the century) which have since become household words, the success of which was due in great part to the classic early campaigns behind them: Bovril (which has supplied us with some of the greatest advertisements of all time), the Millais 'Bubbles' (for Pears' Soap), the early Ovaltine campaigns (sentimental but hard-working), Gillette's first advertisement, a little later, for the safety razor (a masterpiece of simple, selling copy) and, of course, Guinness (strangely enough, a late-comer to the advertising world in 1929) with its marvellously ingenious and varied presentation of its single simple claim, perhaps the most famous slogan in the history of British advertising.

It is interesting to see just how good some of this early advertising

[1] *The New Review* (July 1894).

was, despite the lack of modern tools. There was no research, no media data to speak of, no advertisement testing; yet some of the advertisements would hold their own with any of those produced today for the strength of their presentation and the single-mindedness of their message. The weeping ox gazing at the Bovril jar over the headline 'Alas! my poor brother' can hardly be bettered as a strong and memorable product description, and the famous Sunlight Soap 'Why does a Woman look old sooner than a Man?' needs no motivational research to prove it right.

What is even more interesting and remarkable is that, for the most part, these early advertisements and campaigns were created without the help and advice of an advertising agency; the agency merely supplied the mechanical processes of their production. They were the products, by and large, of dynamic, original thinkers who saw advertising as an inherent part of the business process; these men provided the meat on which the agencies later fed. They showed the way; the growth of the agency followed. They provided the imagination and creativity: the agencies the structure and organisation.

Thus, even from the start of civilisation, man has felt the need to advertise. It has been a part of his relationship with society, a fundamental element in his communication with others. There have, of course, been developments of technique, but the basic principles have remained remarkably constant. Perhaps one of the most significant shifts of emphasis over the centuries has been the transition, in organised advertising, from the artistic to the commercial. Just as in architecture, where there are few, if any, modern equivalents of the Michelangelos, the Berninis and the Wrens who provided the cities of the world with so much grace and beauty, so in advertising we rarely see a latter-day Toulouse-Lautrec, Millais or Aubrey Beardsley providing the artistic content of the modern promotional message.

There are, of course, still to be found some examples of advertising which use illustrations provided by mainly non-commercial artists, but these tend to be very specialised cases, not the central campaign pieces of Millais and Beardsley. Nicolas Bentley and Ronald Searle are typical in this context, but they are cartoonists and are used to particularly good effect when humour or wit are needed. Feliks Topolski used to draw for White Horse Whisky, but his drawings are no longer used. John Piper, Graham Sutherland, Sydney Nolan and Edward Ardizzone have all on occasions turned their attentions to advertising work, but since the 1950s the incidence has declined. Like modern architecture, modern advertising is largely functional, highly skilled but very pragmatic.

Growth of the Agency

The agency grew fast. The J. Walter Thompson Company was founded in 1867, now the largest and most ramified advertising organisation in the world, and the advertising business was gradually coming to an awareness of itself as a significant force in industry. At first, agencies tended to affiliate themselves to particular newspapers or magazines, but it rapidly became apparent that such limitations were inhibiting if the agency was to be able to offer a comprehensive service to its clients, many of whom had national interests far beyond the local or regional spheres of influence that most of the smaller agencies controlled.

It was clear that manufacturers wanted two things above all else: firstly, help and advice on the creation and content of the advertising message, and secondly, help and advice on the choice of media in which to feature it. Thus, the early advertising agencies, almost in spite of themselves, were forced into the situation of having to provide their clients with a *complete* service, consisting of both creative material and media buying, even though no payment for creative services was made. The preparation of advertisement content was, from the beginning, part of the service, paid for (oddly enough) not by the client but by the publication; in the years to come, agencies were to rue the day that such terms of business had ever been permitted, and much of the controversy in modern advertising revolves around this very point, but in the heady days of the advertising gold rush few men paused to think of the implications of such a decision.

During the last three decades of the nineteenth century the industry grew, but it was growth in size, not in scope. Fundamentally, no new developments took place from the day that Carlton and Smith (the original name of J. Walter Thompson) opened its doors until after the Second World War. Advertising budgets increased, naturally, and more and more companies elected to use the services of an advertising agency; but, in terms of operation and structure, agencies remained in principle the same – organisations supplying basically the creative and media needs of their clients. Press media provided the bulk of their business, but outdoor advertising (posters) and, later, radio added to their source of revenue.

There is a sort of amateur look about advertising before 1939. Although it was undoubtedly a part of the business scene it was in a strange way removed from the real and central business process, a satellite, possibly even something of a joke. It had all the connotations of the arts, but not the respectability; and the people who worked in advertising were either the by-products of the newspaper business, or creative writers and artists who would have felt far more respectable at a Foyle's lunch or Burlington House. This engendered an attitude within the industry which was to influence it significantly in later years when it did at last integrate itself more closely with the business function, and still causes it to regard itself as less disreputable and more gentlemanly than the rest of industry.

Few of the people who worked in advertising before the war are in it now. They were a strange breed, doing what they did because perhaps they either could not or would not do anything else. They would be astonished if they could see the sophisticated techniques at work in the industry today, but they would doubtless recognise many of the attitudes which still prevail.

Pre-war advertising was very much a subjective, ideas-in-the-bath type of operation, unsupported by the refinements of motivational research or computer analysis. While Dorothy Sayers's *Murder Must Advertise* is a work of fiction it undoubtedly portrays fairly accurately the behaviour and attitudes prevalent in the 1930s, attitudes summed up pretty acidly by the the 'hunches and lunches' criticism which was regularly levelled at advertising in the early post-war years.

It was this rather carefree, slightly flippant and semi-artistic outlook, more appropriate to the theatre than to the boardroom, which earned for advertising the reputation of glamour that it still has, even with copy typists seeking their first job after leaving secretarial college. In this respect it ranks with television, although in most of its modern functions it can be just as mundane and tedious as any other type of business.

Increasing Sophistication

Since the Second World War, however, advertising, like so many other industries, has undergone a period of great change, partly due to the rapid developments in business technology, but perhaps even more because of a growing feeling on its own part that it needed a fuller and more authoritative involvement in its clients' operations, and the realisation that without a deeper and more comprehensive understanding of all aspects of client activity it could not properly function in the modern marketing climate.

Hence, the 1950s were marked by a tremendous increase of activity within advertising itself, the emphasis being placed very heavily on two areas which, in the sense that they were officially represented departmentally, were new to the majority of agencies – marketing and research. We shall see later how the typical agency functions, and how these two activities fit into the total advertising operation. It is enough to observe here that the rate at which they were introduced into the agency system was almost indecent: no agency could possibly be thought respectable or professional unless it presented itself as 'marketing-orientated'. Whether most of them really knew what marketing is all about is questionable.

The basis upon which this new formula was presented to potential clients was the argument that the agency could now offer a total marketing service. In theory, this meant that the whole process, from new product development to advertising strategy and sales promotion, could be handed over to the agency, which would act as an extension of the client's own marketing division and would be almost as closely integrated into the client company as any of the client's own internal departments. All the techniques of marketing research, of media analysis, of creative planning and of merchandising would be at the client's service at a rate far lower than if he were to employ the personnel himself.

In theory, this was very attractive. In fact, it rarely happened. For one thing, agency service departments, particularly in the areas of marketing and research, often tended to be departments only in name, thinly and amateurishly staffed. For another, the attitude of many agencies (resulting from the historical development of the commission-on-turnover system of remuneration) was that such departments, while giving the agency the proper image of comprehensive service, could only be tolerated if they were profitable in their own right; thus, research was frequently recommended and implemented for the sake of research rather than for the benefits it provided in terms of improved advertising strategy. Naturally enough, being a very short-sighted attitude, it rarely helped either the agency or the client.

This period, lasting roughtly from 1950 to the mid-sixties, was perhaps the zenith of advertising agency organisation. At no other time in their history have advertising agencies been so complex, so heavily staffed, so expensive to run. Fortunately for the business, it was also a time of increasing appropriations and developing industries which demanded more advertising; this meant that, despite the greater complexity and cost of agency overheads, it was still a very profitable business, and many fortunes were made during these years. The agencies grew fat, often on their clients' ignorance. They also became complacent, and sowed the seeds of their future decline.

The boom attracted many men who were conversant with the comparatively new skills of marketing. Industry, largely because it knew no better, was unable to employ them, so they took their opportunities where they could. The agencies welcomed them with open arms because they represented an advantage over their clients which was invaluable, and it was because of this that their services were in such heavy demand. The advertising industry had never known such prosperity before, and certainly never has since.

All this coincided with a growing internationalism in advertising. It was during this period that many of the large American agencies began to develop overseas offices in Europe, in Asia, in Australia, in South Africa and in South America. Led by J. Walter Thompson and McCann-Erickson (the embryo of the modern Interpublic group), the Americans forged an advertising trail across the world. Partly by acquisition, partly by association and partly by opening subsidiary offices in the major capitals, they were able to take advantage of the international ramifications of their larger clients, organisations such as Esso, Coca-Cola, Mars, General Motors, Ford and Nabisco. Startled European offshoots of American parent companies suddenly found themselves assailed by crowds of strange fast-talking advertising men from New York, who laid down the law on creative strategy and product policy; many British advertising agencies which had been swallowed up in the general maelstrom were told that their ideas were out of date and whole campaigns were imported from the other side of the Atlantic, words and all (I remember once having to use American artwork for an advertisement in *Woman's Own* for Revlon lipstick which included the word 'color').

Those agencies which avoided the transatlantic predators in a sense had the best of both worlds: they preserved their independence and at the same time gained experience from the evidence before their eyes. Marketing was the same, whatever the flag under which it sailed, and its weight of shot was stronger than that in anybody else's locker. However, as with so many other elements of British industry, resistance to the force exerted from the United States was only temporary, and now the larger part of organised advertising in this country is American owned.

Return to Basics

On the other hand, such a development in agency organisation had probably been useful. Clients themselves had not been quick to equip themselves with the marketing outlook necessary for the post-war era. Too many of them were still influenced and controlled (indeed, some still are) by the attitudes and outlook of production directors and engineers; too few of them realised that successful business operations began with the accurate identification of consumer or user needs and ended with the satisfaction of those needs by the supply of appropriate products and services.

As a result, the agencies were able to fill to some extent a gap in client expertise and to find a ready market for the new services which they offered. But it must have been clear to most of them that such a situation could not be expected to last for ever. It could only be a matter of time before client companies became better qualified than the agencies themselves to plan and analyse their own marketing requirements; and this is in fact what happened. By 1960 the trend was already evident; by 1965 it was complete, and the agencies found themselves, to a very large degree, duplicating operations which their clients could, if anything, do better.

The situation now, therefore, is that most reputable advertising agencies, while being structured on a so-called 'total service' basis, use their service departments – particularly in the realms of research and marketing – as analyst departments, acting on a brief from either inside or outside the agency, to digest and process information, but not to recommend on future action as they used to several years ago. The driving force, the *raison d'être*, of the modern agency is its ability and experience in defining and identifying advertising – primarily creative – problems, and supplying the imaginative and persuasive strategic thinking which will translate the solution into strong and effective advertising communication. If clients get this they are getting value for money. And furthermore they are very lucky.

Chapter 2

Advertising Today

Advertising and Society

Before examining the structure of modern advertising, it is important to establish the role that advertising plays in our mid-twentieth century world.

There are many critics of advertising, and the criteria of criticism are almost as plentiful as the critics themselves. Advertising is attacked on economic grounds, on moral grounds, on political grounds and on aesthetic grounds, and while all of these criticisms may each contain a grain of justification they none of them succeed in presenting a totally satisfactory case. There is in advertising, of course, much to be criticised, but the faults lie more in the practice than the principle; and there are few activities of which exactly the same comment would not be equally true. All things suffer from abuse.

Economic Argument. John Hobson, the founder of one of Britain's most successful advertising agencies, in a lecture he gave to the Royal Society of Arts a few years ago as President of the Institute of Practitioners in Advertising, put to rights one of the major misconceptions which prevail about advertising:

Advertising is not (as some people seem to imagine) something in its own right, some separate estate of the realm, like civil administration, or the Services, or law. Advertising is an integral and essential part of industry – its projection into the vital department of selling. . . . Advertising reflects industry's intentions and will, its strengths and weaknesses; indeed it does more than reflect them – it projects them on to the biggest screen possible. For the most part British industry's intentions are honest, honourable and fair. Indeed most manufacturers believe implicitly that they have succeeded in making products that are better than the competition in their properties, performance or value. They may sometimes be mistaken, but their belief is honest. This confidence they translate into their advertising.

The first and most important function of advertising, therefore, is to sell. Advertising for toothpaste is designed to sell oral hygiene; advertising for motor cars is selling transport; advertising for life insurance is selling family security; and advertising for charities is selling the satisfaction of social conscience or a warm feeling of generosity.

There is nothing immoral in this; advertising is just one part of the complicated process which begins on the production line and ends in the larder, the bathroom or the garage. Yet the view persists that, while it is perfectly respectable to produce, it is somehow not quite proper to consume; and, since advertising is one of the methods by which consumption is encouraged, it is tainted by this impropriety. But you cannot have one without the other, and, when governments set targets of economic growth expressed in terms of production, they delude themselves if they do not by the same token accept that a corresponding consumer demand must be found for that production; the function of advertising is to help to arouse that demand. As Adam Smith said, 'Consumption is the sole end and purpose of all production.'

A commercially-minded marketing man (as distinct from a government economist) would, of course, express the equation rather differently: he would insist that the process both begins and ends with the consumer; that demand is the stimulus for production; and that without demand no production is justified. But it really all amounts to the same thing: the gap between production and consumption or demand must never be allowed to grow too large, and in this context advertising helps, not only by stimulating demand and raising consumption, but by smoothing out demand fluctuations which make for instability and high costs.

The economic argument for advertising can be taken further. It is maintained in some circles that if there were no advertising the cost of products would be cheaper. This is perfectly true, given the stimulation of sufficient demand to enable production to be carried out on a large enough scale to allow for low unit costs; but it is precisely through advertising that such conditions are created, and advertising, far from increasing the cost of products, actually lowers it by raising the level of demand. Advertising is thus just as necessary a part of the cost of a product as its packaging or the machine on which it was made or the labour required to run that machine.

Those critics who do not entirely condemn advertising are prepared to accept all these arguments in principle, but maintain that although advertising is a necessary part of selling there is far too much of it. They will invariably quote the vast sums spent on the promotion of soap powders and detergents as prime examples of self-defeating and unnecessary effort; this, they say, goes beyond the requirements of the business objective, and should be controlled by law.

While there are admittedly areas of industry which are populated by large numbers of apparently similar and heavily advertised products all competing against each other, it is worth remembering two things. Firstly, the amount of expenditure on advertising, proportionate to the Gross National Product, has not increased significantly since 1938 (in fact since 1961 it has decreased from 1·3 per cent to 1·2 per cent of the GNP); thus, advertising is growing only in the sense that it keeps pace with the development of the affluent society, while the emphasis on many other factors of life in that society has changed dramatically in the last thirty years. Secondly, industry does not spend its millions on advertising merely to amuse itself; it is an undeniable fact that it increases sales by doing so, even in the soap powder and detergent market referred to above, and the net result of increases in sales of competing products is an increase in the total market for those products.

It is true that some product groups grow at a much slower rate than others as a result of many factors, some measurable, some not. One thing, however, is certain: no profit-conscious manufacturer will devote an increasingly large advertising budget to a waning product in a declining market. He will try another market. There are very few examples of products which have been revived once they have reached the decline stage of what marketing men call the 'product life cycle'.

Moral Argument. Advertising, then, must be granted respectability on economic grounds. But what of the moral argument? It is often said that advertising makes people buy what they don't want, that it creates needs and builds an acquisitive society. It is thus accused of exploiting consumer weaknesses and trading on the baser human emotions.

It is questionable whether it is possible to create a need which did not previously exist. On the other hand, it is undeniable that needs can be latent, and that people may not be aware of them until they have been aroused, as has been proved many times by motivational studies carried out by the market researchers. We must, I think, be careful here to distinguish between the need and the satisfaction of the need, between the problem and the product; before the invention of the washing machine, for example, no housewife was aware that she needed such a product, but she was certainly aware that she needed something that would make washing day less of a drudgery.

Also, it is important to be sure that we know the difference between a need and a want; the two terms are frequently confused and employed indiscriminately in discussions of the moral considerations of advertising. Put quite simply, we need to eat, but we do not need to eat caviare; we may want to eat it, but we do not need to. The need allows us a considerable latitude of wants, and in advertising terms this latitude is expressed through the availability of many different branded products in healthy competition with each other.

Some needs, of course, are stronger than others; this brings us back to Maslow's hierarchy of needs (referred to at the beginning of this book). The basic needs of food, drink, shelter, warmth, sex and companionship are self-evident, but it is not so easy to define what kind of need specific products are aiming to satisfy unless we are party to the research which may have probed into the markets for those products. Take a box of chocolates, for instance: on the very basic level, this product answers the need for food, but nobody would argue that it is the most obvious satisfaction of that particular need; the more likely possibilities are that it is answering either a specific desire (or want) for something sweet to eat or a (very common) need to obtain pleasure from giving (Black Magic chocolates have for a long time been promoted on this very premise).

Therefore, when people object to advertising on moral grounds they are in a sense denying freedom of choice. In a capitalistic society it is inconsistent to allow people the opportunity to earn as much money as they can, and then refuse them the right to spend it on whatever they want. Is it wrong, if people want washing machines, for competing manufacturers to offer them a selection of different models in different styles at different prices? Is it wrong, if people are too busy to peel potatoes because the whole family is out at work all day, for a food company to charge a little more than the raw product for the convenience of mashed potato in a packet? Is it wrong, if I have a headache, for me to be offered the choice of aspirin or Paracetamol?

Let us take a more controversial example. It is said that we got on very well without deodorants before they were invented, and that the manufacturers of such products are exploiting our feelings of guilt when they tell us that we should use a deodorant out of consideration for other people. Now it is true that most of us are sensitive to other people's opinion of us; it is also true that some of us have strong, and frequently unpleasant, B.O. It has been proved quite conclusively that many people were self-conscious because of this even before the arrival of deodorants, and this research in fact led to the development of such products.

There is a very important point here. It is the function of modern marketing to identify consumer needs and wants through research and observation, and to provide (in the form of products and services) the means of satisfying those wants. The wants themselves will not always be obvious to the consumer; how often have we heard the remark 'I don't know how I ever managed without it' from somebody who has bought something for the first time? Marketing, through the medium of advertising communication, will relate the want (latent or otherwise) to the satisfaction of it. If there are people (as in the case of deodorants) who choose not to buy the product or service, either because they feel it is not relevant to them or for any other reason, that is their right. But it is equally the right of those people who want it to buy it. An appeal to the feeling of guilt may well be an appeal to a base motive, but the alleviation of that feeling can only be good.

It would be unrealistic to deny that some advertisements offend against accepted moral standards, but they are so few as to be only a minute proportion of the total weight of advertising directed at the public. Most advertising is well within the bounds of moral behaviour, and when people object to it they do so for the most part because it is irrelevant to themselves. All advertisers at times make mistakes; as Hobson says, 'The failures of marketing always reside in the failure to assess rightly whether a true want exists.' In other words, the advertiser's fault lies not in his conscious and deliberate plan to force products down people's throats against their will, but in his relating the wrong product to the wrong consumer and at the same time believing that he is doing the right thing. In so doing he is guilty of nothing more than the errors of judgement to which all of us are prone.

Political Argument. Many criticisms are levelled against advertising by politicians of all parties. The basis for these criticisms is to be found in many different personal interpretations of party ideologies, but their overtones exist in both economic and moral criticism, and it is sometimes difficult to isolate them.

This book is not about political theory, but about an element of business activity, and it is therefore perhaps advisable to avoid party controversy. One point, however, does need to be made: how many, I wonder, of those politicians who publicly state that advertising should be abolished, or taxed, or curtailed, would apply the same strictures to the advertising of their own party? All parties indulge in the activity for their own political ends; indeed, it can be argued that the funds they devote to this in no way represent a true picture of the size of their advertising effort, for all their major speeches are reported in the press and on television, and every day politicians appear on radio and television programmes putting forward their party's view. These days politics appears to be developing into more of a business than business itself, and if some politicians level an accusing finger at advertising (which is a part of the business process) they are at the same time accusing themselves.

At least, advertising for commercial products and services is subject to some fairly stringent controls and is frequently required to substantiate its claims. Were the same obligations incumbent upon the political parties, we might find that election manifestos more often bore a similarity to the performance of governments than they appear to do today. Unlike a tube of toothpaste or a packet of detergent, a government can last for five years, and the only recourse to complaint the consumer has is to wait patiently until the fullness of time provides the opportunity to elect an alternative which, in the event, turns out to be no better than the first.

Aesthetic Argument. Where the critics of advertising are perhaps on their firmest ground is in the argument about the aesthetic standards and the general quality of much of the material we see in our newspapers, on our television screens and on the hoardings. It is undeniable that not every advertisement is an example of good taste; it is equally undeniable that not every advertisement is a literary or artistic masterpiece. But we should be careful not to fall into the error of judging advertising on criteria which are not, after all, its prime terms of reference; people are very ready to say that they dislike an advertisement because it does not meet their own requirements of taste or quality, but they will rarely take the trouble to judge it as an effective selling weapon. They are naturally subjective, and thus fail to appreciate that advertising, by definition, cannot be all things to all men: since advertising is a product of our social environment, it will necessarily mirror all the elements of our society, and those elements will include all tastes.

One only needs to compare the general tone of advertisements in 'class' newspapers with that of those in the more popular press to see how advertising uses the language and interests of differing press readership to appeal to particular types of people. Thus you find that, generally speaking, advertisements in, say, the *Guardian* will be couched in rather different terms and will advertise rather different products from advertisements in the *Sun* or the *Daily Mirror* (I say 'generally speaking' because there are, of course, many products which are universally advertised and equally attractive to all classes).

The central point is that, while there are admittedly a few examples of advertisements which reduce standards of taste and literary quality to an intolerably low level, advertising for the most part will approach its audience in language and presentation appropriate to the occasion, just as your favourite newspaper does for you. Because of the wide differences of character, environment, upbringing, income and location, it is extremely difficult to communicate successfully to everybody in similar terms, and you can be reasonably sure that, if you find an advertisement vulgar, badly written or irrelevant, it was never meant for you in the first place.

Social Effects of Advertising. We have examined the economic, moral and aesthetic context of advertising, but we have not yet touched on the question of its social implications. Advertising is very much a part of our social scene; indeed, we have seen how its growth has been a direct result of changes and developments in society itself. Our everyday life would seem dramatically different were there no advertisements, so different in fact that it is virtually impossible to conceive of such a condition.

If, therefore, advertising is so integral a part of our existence, what effects has it had on the way we live? How has this social phenomenon affected society itself?

It has influenced society in three major ways. Firstly, it has undoubtedly improved our general standard of living; not entirely on its own, it is true, but it has contributed enormously. Mass production, which allows goods to be manufactured cheaply, is made possible largely through the demand stimulated by advertising; improved technology and better products are benefits which result from mass production. This rise in living standards owes other things to advertising: an ever-growing awareness of hygiene, of health standards and safety precautions, to mention only three of the most significant benefits. Despite growing uniformity, which naturally involves the lowering of some standards and the raising of others, men and women in Britain today regard as commonplace the possessions and activities which even thirty years ago a previous generation looked on as unattainable luxuries. It is partly to the power of modern advertising that this affluent society is due.

The second effect of advertising is a result, or rather a less desirable aspect, of the first. Society, while enjoying high living standards, has become much more materialistic in its outlook. It is difficult to see how it could have been prevented from becoming so, since the escape from poverty and the acquisition of luxury is a continuous process without defined lines of demarcation. If it is right to give people spending power, it is not equally right that they should have a wide choice of material benefits on which to spend?

In any case, it is not the materialism and acquisitiveness themselves which are regrettable, but the effect that these tend to have on what (for want of a better term) we call the 'quality of life'. The countryside is scarred by miles of motorway, desperately trying to cope with an ever-increasing flood of motor cars; seas and rivers are polluted to danger levels in the cause of production; fields and woods are sprinkled with the bottles and cartons of countless picnics; and ears are shattered by jet aircraft carrying their passengers on packaged tours to Morocco or Majorca. All these are to a greater or smaller degree due to the changing social forces inspired by the materialistic age in which we live, and while advertising may only be a small part of the total picture it stands out clearly on the canvas.

Perhaps the most dangerous effect of advertising, however, is the change it has made in the emphasis of power. We saw in the first chapter how the industrial revolution provided the conditions in which advertising was able to develop and thrive, and it is undoubtedly to industry that advertising has been the greatest use. In the process of increasing its turnover, its efficiency and its profitability, in the process of pushing up living standards and creating an affluent society, in the process of developing the technology with which wars are won and lost, industry has, by its extensive and continuous use of modern communications, become the greatest single influence on the social scene. While this has not yet become a dangerous influence, it is theoretically possible for industry (or parts of industry) to make it so, and there is thus a heavy responsibility on its shoulders. Let us hope it can carry it.

The Art of Communication

Many people have attempted to produce formulas and philosophies for effective advertising. In a way, this is not only a dangerous but also a rather arrogant thing to do, because the formulas work only some of the time.

We have seen that advertising is the communication of sales propositions; it holds no brief to be funny, arty or clever. It needs only to achieve reaction on the part of its audience which will lead to a purchase of the products it presents; and advertising must conform to certain basic requirements if it is going to achieve this.

It must, firstly, speak to *the right people*. In the previous section we argued that advertisements which were ignored, derided or abused were likely to be directed at people other than those who ignored, derided or abused them. This is the fundamental principle of advertising communication – accurate audience definition.

Secondly, it must speak to its defined audience through *appropriate media*. It is no use using *The Times* to reach the working class, or the *Daily Mirror* to reach lawyers, doctors and managing directors. As McCluhan says, 'the medium is the massage' (which means, despite its frequent misinterpretation, merely that unless you speak through the right channels the best message in the world means nothing at all).

Thirdly, the message itself must be *appropriate to its audience* in several ways. It must be couched in language which the audience can understand; it must appeal to feelings, either latent or obvious, which the audience is known to have; and it must offer a real benefit expressed in comprehensible terms. Furthermore, it must succeed in establishing contact with the audience's mind quickly, simply and effectively.

There is no single golden rule for achieving these objectives. The considerations affecting any two advertising problems will be different, and therefore the means which are employed to solve them will be different. The people who create advertisements, of course, will build up their own rules based on experience; they will know which approaches are likely to be successful in a given situation and which unsuccessful; they know that audiences, in the words of Mark Abrams (a well-known expert in communications research), are not just 'a passive blank', but complex storehouses of attitudes and interests which must be stimulated and aroused by the message.

Leslie Rodger,[1] in his excellent book, analyses the communication process by balancing the elements of communication against the business of communication, and shows how the two are in constant conflict as the advertiser tries to pull the consumer through the stages of awareness,

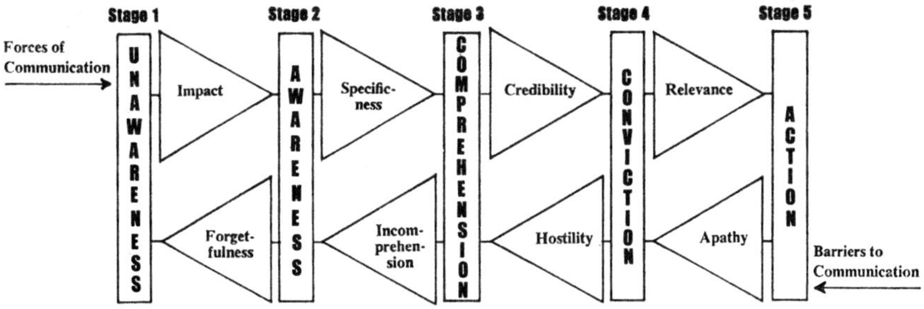

Fig. 1 A modified brand loyalty ladder

comprehension, conviction and action (leading to purchase). Much the same conflict is expressed in Philip Kotler's[2] 'brand loyalty ladder', on which the marketing effort (and, in particular, advertising) attempts to lift the consumer from the bottom rung to the top, through the successive stages of brand awareness, brand knowledge, brand preference and brand

[1] Leslie W. Rodger, *Marketing in a Competitive Economy* (Hutchinson, 1965), p. 183.
[2] Philip Kotler, *Marketing Management: Analysis, Planning and Control* (Prentice-Hall, 1972), p. 465.

loyalty, against the downward forces of communications and sales barriers. While these illustrations show the general problem, neither of them shows how progress achieved by effective advertising can be impaired at specific stages along the line; for instance, it is possible to postulate a kind of snakes-and-ladders picture of the ups and downs of advertising at work on the consumer's mind (see Fig. 1).

Naturally, the forces and barriers illustrated in Fig. 1 are by no means exhaustive. The really essential qualities of effective advertising, including those illustrated, are:

1. *Impact:* the advertisement must attract attention.
2. *Relevance:* it must be appropriate to the needs of the person at whom it is directed.
3. *Single-mindedness (specificness):* it must not only be specific in the message it presents, but must also try to concentrate on a single selling proposition; too many advertisements try to say too much and thus lack a focus for audience attention and memory.
4. *Reason:* its selling message must be backed by an authoritative justification, e.g. 'Presto saves you money *because* you get more in every packet.'
5. *Credibility:* the proposition presented must be believable, either factually ('0–60 m.p.h. in 8 seconds') or emotionally ('makes you feel ten feet tall').
6. *Topicality:* the message must be appropriate to its audience in time and place.
7. *Identity:* the advertisement must indicate the identity of the product, service or company advertised clearly, quickly and easily.

In the same way, we can list those factors which can militate against the success of an advertisement (other, of course, than a lack of those attributes indicated above):

1. *Apathy:*	consumer laziness, indifference or inertia.
2. *Hostility:*	consumer rejection of or antipathy to the proposition presented.
3. *Incomprehension:*	lack of understanding of the proposition or its relevance.
4. *Forgetfulness:*	loss of memory of the proposition.
5. *Competitive activity:*	stronger propositions presented by competing advertising.
6. *Unfavourable market conditions:*	changes in the structure and character of the market, such as lower income, death, etc.
7. *Product similarity:*	too many similar products with indistinguishable advertising claims in the same market.

Many advertisements fall short of the specifications which have been listed; all advertisements can be improved, of course, but some are bad from birth. The reason is that the people who have created them have been preoccupied with the visual details to the detriment of the central theme, and in most cases bad advertising is guilty because it lacks two of the listed specifications in particular – single-mindedness and identity. Take, for instance, the following four examples seen in a London tube train at the same time from the same seat (in all, ten advertisements were visible):

'You needn't be rough to be smooth' (no brand name was visible, and the fact that the advertised product was a hair remover became apparent only after a long and careful scrutiny of small print; there was no illustration to help with the explanation).

'Wanted' (illustration: two open cigarette packs, sideways on, no brand name visible; the headline was incomprehensible without an examination of the small body copy, in which the brand name was buried).

'Some girls don't know when to stop' (an intriguing headline, it is true, but baffling in the absence of a brand name, especially when it was discovered, from long copy, to be Barclays Bank).

'Hello Dolly' (no brand name identifiable at all, even after protracted perusal).

The advertisers who paid for these advertisements might just as well have saved their money.

How different, however, is the advertisement featured in Plate 8 for Cadbury's Drinking Chocolate. The presentation has impact, the proposition has relevance and is very specific, credible and topical; above all, the advertisement gives the product an immediate and memorable identity. The whole effect is simple and clear, and represents advertising communication at its very best.

There are many home-made do's and don'ts which some advertising people observe slavishly and which others realise to be rules capable of being effectively broken when the situation demands, namely: 'A positive headline is better than a negative one', or 'Black lettering on white is better than white lettering on black', and the best one of all, salutary and ominous:

> Should the client prove refractory,
> Show a picture of his factory;
> But only in the gravest case
> Show a picture of his face.

These so-called errors are committed every day, and the results are frequently perfectly acceptable.

In general, advertising falls into two categories: immediate effect advertising and delayed effect advertising. These categories have been variously described by other names which, in addition to being less accurate, are also rather confusing, such as 'hard sell/soft sell' or 'product/image' or 'product/prestige': these latter descriptions seem to suggest that there can be a sort of advertising which is not designed to sell anything, as if manufacturers sometimes spend their money merely to see their name in the papers.

Immediate effect advertising is self-explanatory: it is designed to achieve immediate sales (of toothpaste, frozen food or ladies' fashions). Delayed effect advertising is more complex; it, also, is designed to achieve sales but in different ways. By a gradual build-up of public awareness of a product's quality or a company's reputation for design, service or technical ability in markets where purchases are relatively infrequent (such as motor cars, life insurance or household durables) it is hoped to establish a brand image and a loyalty potential which will be realised when the purchase is eventually made. It is sometimes difficult to see the value of extreme examples of this (those impressive half-pages in *The Times* and *The Financial Times* for BAC or Pilkington Glass or ICI) since they are not directed at their audience as individuals but as members of airline companies, building contractors and other industrial organisations. The description 'prestige advertising' in cases such as this is understandable but misleading. *All* advertising is selling advertising; advertisements differ only in the time-scale of their effects, and the longer the time-scale the more difficult it is to evaluate those effects.

In a sense, advertising sells ideals with which its audience can identify itself; the psychological associations of a man with his motor car, of a woman with her lipstick are obvious; that is why cars and cosmetics are so often sold in emotive terms, and on promises of fantasy ('the lazy fireball' or 'the touch of paradise'). Even mundane and material items such as canned food or garden equipment are presented on an appeal to people's private aspirations – to be the mother who is praised by her family for the wonderful meals she serves or the man of the soil communing with nature (as he digs and mows his suburban back garden on a Sunday afternoon).

It is this emotive factor in advertising which largely contributes towards the building up of the *brand image* (the term used to describe the way in which a product or a company is regarded in the public mind) which is the criterion on which buying decisions are made. Other factors contribute too, of course – packaging, performance, price and retail display – but advertising, because of its wide coverage and power of communication, is naturally the greatest single influence. It is a product's (or company's) *image* which differentiates it from competing products in the market place, and once an image has been strongly established it is difficult, if not impossible, to change it (as will be seen in the Double Diamond example which is quoted later in this chapter).

In the end, the important fact to remember about advertising communication is that the audience is much less close to the problem than the advertiser. The consumer is under no obligation to read advertisements; he must be attracted and convinced by technique. What is more, while to the advertiser his advertisement is the most important part of the newspaper, magazine, television screen or hoarding where it appears, to the consumer it is only one of a thousand elements from which he can select to read or listen. The advertiser must, therefore, above everything, try to put himself in the consumer's shoes, and judge his own effort on its competitive merits. Only then will he know the truth, for the customer is always right.

Agency Structure and Operation

The first chapter traced the evolution of advertising from its beginnings to the present day, and showed how its later history was very much the growth of the advertising agency. The time has now come to examine in some detail how agencies are organised and what they do.

Size and Profitability. Advertising agencies today differ greatly from each other, both in size and structure; there are hundreds in Britain alone, but of these only a handful is of any real importance.

About 80 per cent of total advertising spending goes through the top twenty-five agencies, since, generally speaking, it is the large agencies which attract the large clients. Furthermore, the trend in recent years has been for agencies, like other types of businesses, to merge into larger and larger units in order to economise on the unprofitable services which they have felt bound to offer. A typical example is the Interpublic organisation (made up of McCann-Erickson, Pritchard Wood and Erwin Wasey), and there are many others. Average net profit levels have fallen dramatically from around 2·8 per cent in 1965 to about 1·8 per cent today, reflecting the limitations of the commission system as a method of payment in a climate of rising costs and salaries (an agency's standard commission is 15 per cent).

Most agencies have relatively little working capital, and frequently need the support of the bank to see them through that period between money out and money in, which recurs every month. They have no assets other than the skills of their staff, no guarantees for the future other than the three months' notice their clients are bound to give them, and no sympathy from the media owners (the press and television in particular) if a client goes bankrupt before paying his bill. They are middlemen, dependent entirely on outside forces over which they have little control.

This dependence makes them very vulnerable, particularly in the modern climate of large industrial complexes, to attacks from agencies which are financially better based and expansionist-minded. Their cash flow problem means that their assets can be measured only by the goodwill of their clients, and thus the takeover has become a popular form of new business acquisition. The consequences (both to staff and client relationships) have frequently been severe, and the IPA has, as a result, tried to stimulate an improved cash flow situation in order to avoid too many cases of this kind.

The reduction of profit levels indicates the extent to which the industry has suffered in the economic recession of the late 1960s. During such periods, clients are more than usually cost-conscious, and since as yet no satisfactory correlation has been produced between advertising expenditure and sales results (and it is doubtful if it ever will) it is normally the advertising budget which is reduced before any other. There is, economically speaking, a strong argument to be advanced for *increasing* advertising expenditure at times of depressed demand, but very few manufacturers have ever been brave enough to put it to the test.

The size of agencies varies from those with a staff of several hundreds, and a turnover (or 'billing') of many millions, to those consisting of only two or three people, relying largely on freelance creative services, with a turnover of under £100,000. Some of the smaller agencies may, in order to increase their attractiveness to clients in a particular field, develop a special expertise in specific types of products; this is usually the case with agencies concentrating on industrial products, but it also happens with different types of consumer products to some extent, such as consumer durables or pharmaceuticals.

However, when we talk about the 'typical' advertising agency, we are usually referring to those handling the bulk of the nation's advertising, the top twenty or thirty, the difference between which is one merely of size. Organisationally, they are similar (see Fig. 2), if not identical, and they all have a portfolio of clients which constitutes a fairly representative sample of the consumer products industries and services we see advertised in our newspapers and on our television screens.

Let us therefore examine in some detail what happens in the 'typical' agency.

The Account Group. By definition, an advertising agency's main concern is the proper servicing of its client's business; thus the focal point of the organisation is the account group, which is responsible for maintaining full and constant contact on all matters between client and agency. Depending on the size of the agency, and consequently the size of its billing and the number and complexity of its accounts, the numbers and strength of the account groups will vary: no hard and fast rules can be laid down for the amount of billing any one person or group of people can handle (advertising men know only too well that it is frequently more difficult, demanding, costly and time-consuming to handle a billing of £50,000 than one of £500,000), but, generally speaking, the greater the turnover the greater the numbers of staff required to handle it.

An account group will normally consist of an account group head (probably a director of the company), assisted by several account executives who may in turn be organised on a seniority basis (account supervisors, senior executives, juniors, assistants, etc.), and who will be individually responsible to the account group head for the administration of their own specific accounts. The normal agency will contain one or more of these groups, whose responsibilities will be to the board of the company either directly or through a director in charge of client service.

The loyalty of the account groups is a very delicate one: on the one hand, they must clearly represent the best interests of their clients; on the other, they are bound to perform their functions to the greatest profit of the agency. The two obligations frequently conflict, and account directors thus often find themselves at variance with their own board colleagues; this is possibly one of the reasons why politics play such an important part in the operation of the average agency, and why there is such a high turnover of senior staff.

The function of the account group (and primarily the function of the account group head) is twofold: firstly, the client's problems and requirements must be properly understood and translated into an intelligible and relevant brief or problem summary for the rest of the agency, so that the appropriate action can be taken and a satisfactory recommendation produced; secondly, the proposals which are evolved must not only meet with the approval of the agency's 'Plans Board' or 'Review Board' (which is an official body appointed to vet all major plans and campaigns), but must also be drawn up in such a way as to constitute a presentable package for the account group to lay before its client with confidence and conviction. As may be imagined, this is a difficult and sometimes irreconcilable task; the irony is that, if things go well, the agency as a whole gets the credit, but, if they don't, the account group is held to ransom.

The good account executive is a man who can constantly re-examine the marketing environment of his client's activity and, by the identification of promotional opportunities, provide the stimuli for intelligent and accurate thinking from his creative and media colleagues. He will also, as and when required, call for further information to clarify particular problems by enlisting the help of marketing analysts and research specialists within the agency, although, since in the case of the latter this will probably involve expenditure through an outside field research organisation, he will require the authority of his client for the allocation of funds for this purpose.

This raises another important aspect of account group responsibility, the control and management of clients' budgets. Ideally, these are set as a result of a detailed evaluation of the cost of achieving defined and agreed advertising objectives; in practice, they are more often than not laid down by the client at the beginning of the financial year on the basis of what is affordable. In either event, it is the function of the account group to see that they are strictly adhered to and that they are exceeded only by special agreement. Furthermore, the accurate control of budgets is essential for the purpose of forecasting turnover, profits and borrowing requirements. This is discussed in greater detail later in this chapter (see *Campaign Control*).

Other Departments. The account group is thus the focal point of agency activity; it originates work, programmes it and co-ordinates the efforts of all other departments. The functions of these departments will become evident in the following description of campaign planning, implementation and control; Fig. 2 illustrates an agency's basic organisational structure, the most important components of which, besides the account group, are:

Creative department: consisting of groups or units of copywriters and art directors, often with visualisers (layout artists) and other copywriters to assist them, television writers, the main studio, and possibly

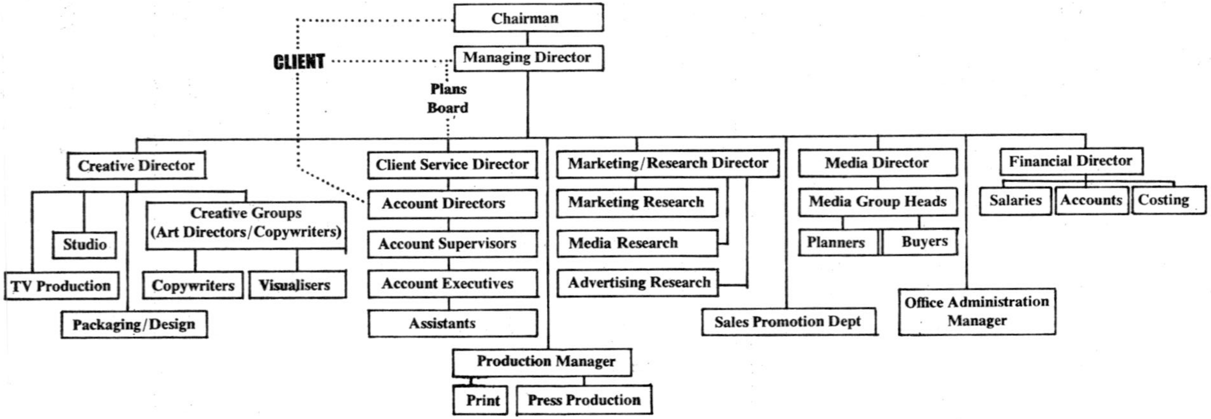

Fig. 2 Organisational structure of a typical agency

N.B. The board of directors will normally consist of the chairman, managing director, creative director, media director, client service director, marketing/research director, financial director and one or more account directors. Responsibility for the production, sales promotion and office administration functions will usually be vested in one of the board members.

	a special unit for packaging and miscellaneous design; television production is frequently responsible to the creative director also.
Media department:	consisting of groups of media planners and buyers, responsible for the formulation of media plans and the booking of agreed schedules.
Marketing research department:	responsible for the provision of marketing information, particularly marketing research, media (readership and viewership) research and advertising research.
Print/production department:	responsible for the implementation of all production of press advertisements and the preparation and buying of print (other than press advertising), e.g. leaflets, posters, point-of-sale display material, etc.
Sales promotion department:	responsible for the preparation and implementation of merchandising activity, and special promotions.
Finance department:	responsible for all accounting activity, including salaries, invoicing and costing.
Office administration:	responsible for the day-to-day administration of the agency, including cleaning, maintenance and junior office staff.

Campaign Planning

The preparation of an advertising campaign is a fairly lengthy process (as can be seen from Fig. 3, which attempts to indicate the pattern of activity involved), and it can begin anything up to twelve months before the first advertisement appears. In this sense, the advertisement itself is merely the tip of the iceberg which protrudes out of the deep waters of much elaborate, and sometimes frenzied, activity.

This activity will normally begin with the briefing, by the client, of all the relevant details of marketing information for the period to be covered, such as sales targets, budgets, new product policy, sales pro-

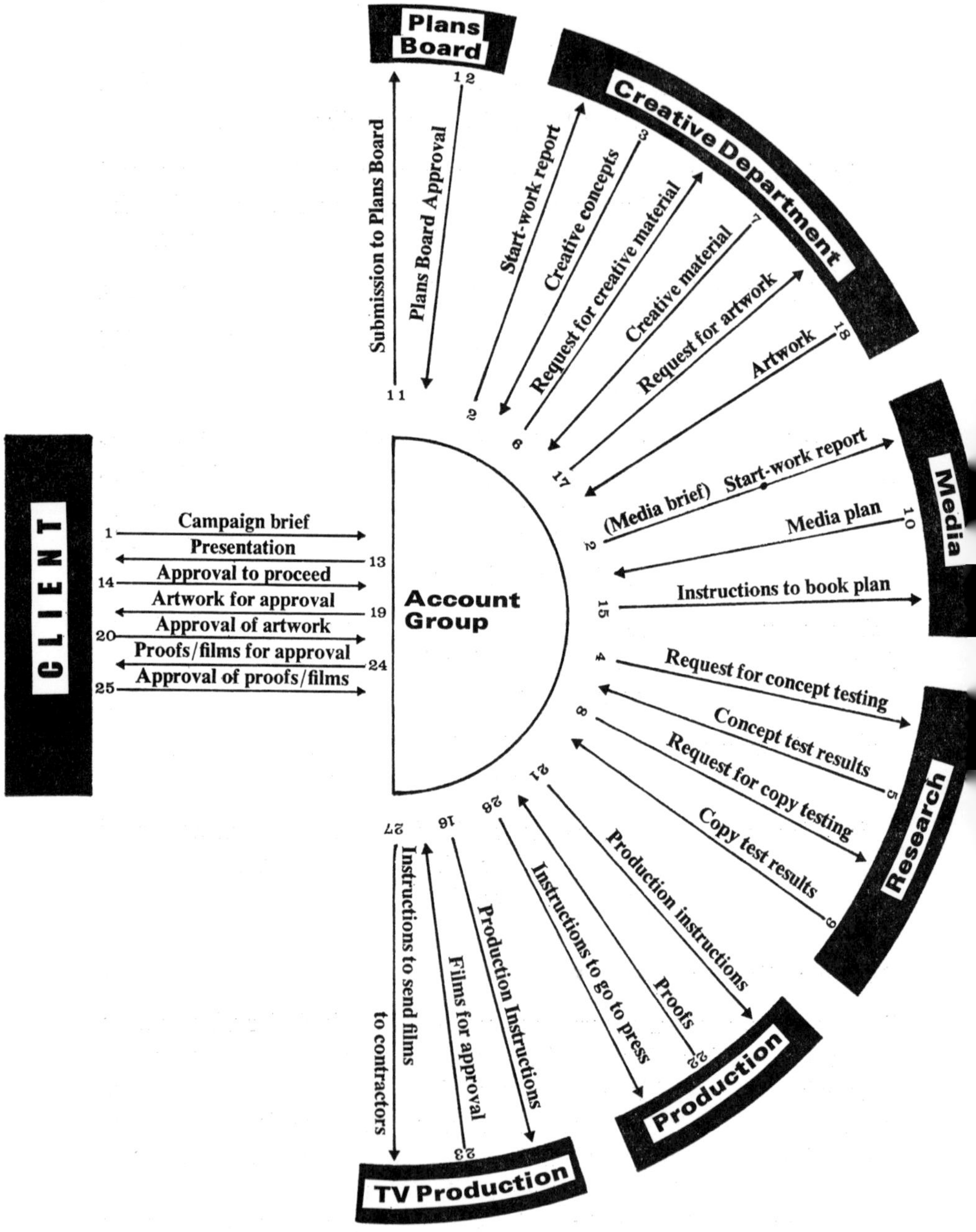

Fig. 3 Typical campaign flow chart

N.B. Physical distribution of material between departments is the responsibility of the traffic department.

motion (point-of-sale) requirements, packaging, research data, and the rest – in short, any information which can in any way affect advertising strategy.

Of course, some (perhaps most) of this the agency will know already, since good client contact is a continuous activity which constantly feeds information back from the client, to be assimilated and acted upon as a matter of course, but a briefing meeting helps to get both sides thinking on agreed lines. Such a meeting will usually consist only of the client's marketing management team and the agency's account group, although it frequently happens that creative or media specialists from other agency departments will attend for specific reasons.

After the meeting, the account group will translate the client's brief into a start-work report, which will summarise the current situation and itemise the objectives which have been set, indicating the work required from different departments for the preparation of the agency's recommendations. Discussions will be held with individual departments, at which verbal amplification of these requirements will be made.

This is a critical stage in the preparation process, since much creative effort can be wasted in the production of excellent material which is totally useless because it does not answer the client's brief. The best instructions from an account group are those which, while pinpointing precisely the area on which to concentrate, do not at the same time inhibit fresh and imaginative ideas through being over-restrictive.

Research for Campaign Planning. There are occasions, at the initial campaign planning stage, when vital information is needed which does not exist. Many references will be made in this chapter to the techniques of research which are involved both in advertisement testing and the evaluation of results; it is perhaps opportune to draw attention here, very briefly, to the methods by which information is gathered to help in the formulation of advertising policy. This clearly is of particular relevance to the launching of new products into new markets, about which clients may not be as well informed as they are in the case of established products.

The future profitability of any company, particularly those companies engaged in the marketing of consumer goods, depends upon its ability to tailor its product range to the changing needs of the market. This postulates a constant re-examination of the suitability of existing products and, even more important, a continuous examination of the possibilities for new product development. Various estimates have been made of the proportion of turnover in consumer goods which will be accounted for in ten years' time by products which do not yet exist, ranging from 20 per cent to 75 per cent, depending on the product group.

Furthermore, from analyses conducted by the A. C. Nielsen Co., it has been estimated that 88 per cent of new products in the American grocery business, for example, turn out to be commercial failures either before or after they have been test marketed. The importance of accurate marketing information, therefore, is evident.

Most, if not all, sophisticated consumer goods manufacturers, of course, will conduct their own new product development programmes, closely linked with manufacturing research and development activity. The advertising agency will thus be consulted only when a new product idea has passed all its initial screening procedures and exists in at least prototype form. Therefore, the agency's marketing research department will be called upon primarily to supply information which will contribute to the communication (as distinct from the product formulation) process. *A fortiori*, this is even more true of established products.

The types of information which the agency may be asked to supply, or may itself wish to discover, fall into three main areas:

1 *Market analysis* (*desk research*). Much information already exists in published form about specific markets and their characteristics, and needs only to be sought out and analysed. Many official and commercial sources of information are readily available in the form of government statistics, reference directories, newspapers, journals and magazines. It is usually possible to discover, from these sources, basic data about market size, potential and trends, and often information about the performance of specific products in a particular market. Information may also be found relating to the demographic (age, class, sex, location) patterns of consumer buying habits and attitudes, though this is less likely.

2 *User market research* (*field research*). Where it is necessary to provide market information which cannot be obtained by desk research, it must be sought from the market itself. This will involve field research involving a structured sample of typical consumers, chosen either on a quota or random basis, and a questionnaire designed to elicit information from these consumers about their buying habits (brands, quantities, frequency and source of purchase, prices paid, etc.).

3 *User attitude research* (*field research*). In addition to facts, effective communication depends on the accurate identification of consumer atttudes and opinions. This also will necessitate field research, either through a consumer survey on the same basis as the one in point 2 above, or through group discussions, where a small number (usually about eight) of consumers is asked, under the supervision of a trained psychologist, to talk in depth about the subject under investigation. Research into consumer attitudes, opinions and motivations, since it involves the evaluation of much subjective judgement, is a highly skilled research technique and requires careful planning and a deep understanding of human psychology.

Both types of field research are carried out through specialist outside research organisations, commissioned for the purpose by the agency. Some of the larger agencies have their own subsidiary research companies.

The clear message emerging from all this is the basis of the marketing function itself: all business activity stems from the consumer (or, in the case of industrial products, the user) and ends with the consumer. Marketing (and advertising) success depends on the accurate identification of user needs and the controlled and systematic process of satisfying those needs. This is why it is impossible for a company to operate satisfactorily without knowledge of its customers, and why so many new products die in infancy.

Creative Concepts. When all the relevant information has been assembled, and all agency departments briefed on the problem, by far the most important decision to be taken will be the selection of the creative concept, the campaign idea, the 'brand placement' as it is sometimes called.

The concept will be the cornerstone of the campaign; it will not be an advertisement or even a headline. It will be the way in which the focus of creative work is described. For example, the concept of promoting a brand of chocolates as gifts (as distinct from the alternative concepts of variety, cream content, glamour or price) will lead eventually to a campaign based on themes such as 'Flatter her with . . .' rather than 'More centres to choose from'.

The value of the creative concept is obvious: it both helps to produce better creative work through the concentration of creative effort on a single area and saves time and effort which would otherwise be wasted on irrelevant themes.

Some concepts are more obvious and easier to agree than others, some may even need to be validated by consumer research, and in some cases consumer research will have to be employed in order to *discover* the concept itself; it may not be possible, for instance, to decide without research that it is more desirable to promote a brand of television set on style than on any other concept – price, size or reliability. One thing is, however, certain, and has been proved in practice often: no concept will work unless it is consistent with what the consumer wants.

Thus, it is the account group's job to produce a definition of objectives with some clear guidelines for creative effort. The actual work of expressing the agreed concept in headlines, pictures and film storyboards will be the responsibility of the creative department, under their creative director, who will start by thinking in very broad terms across several possible alternative methods of implementation. These basic ideas may be little more than pencil scribbles with a headline, or a very rough television commercial suggestion; they will be more the ideas of the writer than the artist (a distinction we shall examine in some detail in Chapter 3), and will represent the candidate list from which more elaborate finished ideas can be developed.

Creative Material. After these suggestions have been discussed with the account group, and agreement reached upon which ones to take to a more finished stage, the creative department will begin to produce material for real advertisements, finished layouts in colour or monotone (employing either photography or careful artists' impressions) and detailed scripts and storyboards for television or cinema commercials. There may be only one campaign or several alternatives (generally speaking, agencies feel more confident when they do not confront their clients with a choice) but in all respects – illustrations, lettering, copy, etc. – they will consist of as close as possible an approximation to the advertisement as it would eventually appear in print or on film. (Examples of advertisement layouts and the corresponding finished advertisements based on them are illustrated in Plates 9 and 10.)

Advertisement Testing. This creative material will represent one part of the agency's recommendation to its client, and will (although the description of the process involved has been very brief) be the result of endless discussions, arguments, modifications and tests. It is usual (certainly in the larger agencies), for instance, for all creative work to be subjected to as much validation as possible through advertisement research, in order to limit the risk of budget expenditure on inappropriate campaigns. Testing will normally be carried out at two stages in the preparation of creative work: firstly at the concept stage, and secondly at the layout (in the case of a press advertisement) or pilot film (in the case of screen material) stages (copy testing).

Concept testing attempts to establish whether or not the basic idea on which a campaign is founded (such as 'High Speed Gas' or 'You can't tell Stork from Butter') is acceptable, believable and relevant to the consumers to whom it will eventually be directed. No advertisements exist at this stage; certainly, it is not the purpose of such research to test them. The research will concentrate (probably through techniques such as group discussions or repertory grids[1]) on fundamental consumer attitudes towards the campaign idea in relation to the type of product involved.

Copy testing is very much more specific; it tries to measure the degree to which a particular advertisement or campaign is effectively communicating the concept. This is normally done through folder tests of press material and audience measurement (in specially equipped theatres) of films; and it will take into consideration virtually every detail of advertisement content.

Thus, for example, when Be-Ro flour (the second RHM brand) was positioned in the market against McDougalls ('Super-sifted to bake super light') and Spiller's Homepride ('Graded grains make finer flour') as the flour which allayed the housewife's anxiety while the cake was cooking, it was first of all necessary to establish that a significant anxiety level existed. Concept research showed that 35 per cent of all housewives admitted to having anxious moments while the cake was in the oven, and (even more importantly) that 74 per cent thought that other women felt this way. When, on the basis of this evidence, the

[1] The Kelly Repertory Grid technique uses group discussions between articulate respondents to establish the criteria upon which concepts (or products) are judged, and subsequently employs a large random sample to rate specific concepts (or products) against these criteria on a series of semantic differential scales. Scores are also rated for ideal measures as a control.

agency produced television commercials showing housewives in this predicament and offering Be-Ro as 'The flour that cuts out oven doubt', they first of all tested them in pilot form and found that housewives readily associated the situations which were portrayed in the commercials with their own personal cooking experiences. The campaign was thus supported by research at both stages, and, when it was run, proved to be very successful for Be-Ro.

Media Planning. The second part of the agency's presentation will be its recommendations on how the client's money will be spent – the media strategy and schedule. Again, this will result from a detailed brief from the account group to the media department. This brief may or may not be so specific as to indicate in what major medium the appropriation is to be employed (press, television, cinema, posters, etc.), but it will certainly ask the media planners to decide on how best to achieve the stated advertising objectives, which are, in turn, a part of the total marketing objective of the client.

Normally, it will be reasonably obvious whether the budget is to be spent in press or television media – the two major choices facing media planners – since this will be influenced partly by the amount of money available and partly by the creative considerations for the campaign. Some products will require demonstration – far easier on the moving screen than in static photography – and certain advertisements will need lengthy explanatory copy, which cannot satisfactorily be contained in a short (sometimes thirty or fifteen seconds) television commercial and will be far more appropriate to a press treatment. Furthermore, it is traditionally more expensive to build up an effective campaign at a low cost on television than in the press.

Whether or not the media planner has to take the fundamental decision on the choice of media group – press, television, posters, cinema, radio, etc. – his major problem will inevitably exist within that medium itself. In the case of television, it will be a matter of deciding (bearing in mind the various creative constraints) how many spots of what length over what period and on what stations can justifiably be planned. His brief will help to some extent, but the problem – the micro-scheduling problem, as it has sometimes been called – is his alone; it is largely a problem of weighing the advantages of coverage (the number of people watching a given television spot) against those of frequency (the number of times the commercial can be transmitted). Costs for off-peak viewing will be cheaper than peak periods, and greater frequency will therefore be possible, but at such times audiences will be lower. Similarly, high audience ratings can be achieved during expensive peak hours, but frequency will suffer. The answer will lie in a judicious balance between the two, so as to achieve the maximum frequency combined with the highest cumulative (i.e. built up over the campaign) coverage.

Exactly the same problems exist in the planning of a press schedule. Some publications have a higher readership than others, and their cost is therefore that much more expensive; by and large, in media terms, you get what you pay for. Again, some publications will be biassed towards particular age or class groups, or to one sex or the other. Some will circulate more extensively, geographically speaking, than others; some will be purely local or regional, others national, and even amongst the latter the distribution patterns will differ tremendously. Thus, the *Daily Telegraph* tends to concentrate its sales into south-eastern England, the *Daily Mirror* is almost non-existent in Scotland (while the *Daily Express* is strong), and in the north-east (particularly on Tyneside) the local press, in coverage terms, is stronger than the national newspapers.

Thus, the problems facing the media planner are by no means as straightforward as they may appear to the layman. Traditionally, the task of media selection has been accomplished through a blend of intuition and experience, using such published information as may exist on the audiences, readership and profiles of the media available. Nowadays, things are becoming rather more scientific; the computer is being brought more and more into the picture, not, it must be said, as a replacement for judgement, but as a means of reducing the very high margins of error which can (and do) creep into schedule analysis.

Faced, for instance, with the problem of drawing up a suitable plan based on a selection of national press media, the planner will first of all make a list of all the possible 'candidate' publications, which will be far more than he can possibly afford, but which will exhaust the opportunities of reaching the defined target market. The readership characteristics of these publications (obtained by national research by the IPA on a representative sample basis) will previously have been fed into a computer, so that by setting the appropriate programme (consisting of a definition of the target audience in terms of age, sex, class, area, desired frequency and coverage, space sizes, etc.) the planner can obtain, comparatively quickly (and far more accurately than ever before), a schedule based on the additional value of each individual publication. He will thus be able to work out the relationship between the real cost of using a given publication and the unduplicated extra value that that publication adds to all the other publications under consideration.

The media planner will thus have used his judgement in the selection of the original list of candidate media (the area where judgemental factors always have been of crucial importance), and in the imposition of the constraints under which the schedule must be compiled – frequency, space size, and so on; but he will have brought a far more highly accurate and analytical method to bear on the compilation of his final schedule than was ever possible in the past.

Television planning is similarly mathematical, in that schedule optimisation (once the fundamental decisions about choice of medium, selection of stations and length of advertisement have been taken) will be largely a matter of the analysis of cumulative audiences as the result of particular frequency and time-segment patterns, based on the audience data provided by daily research carried out by AGB.

The outcome of this activity will be the media plan, which will constitute the remainder of the account group's presentation to its client. The plan will be itemised in as much detail as possible, usually with full supporting analytical data to substantiate the selection of specific media groups or items. Media recommendations are frequently based on fine differences between one possibility and another, perhaps on as little as 1 per cent coverage of a particular target audience; it can be argued that at such tolerances differentiation is invalid, but the agency is required to make a positive proposal on one side or the other and it can only follow the available evidence.

Merchandising Material. Having thus satisfactorily resolved the two major problems – the creative and media strategy – the agency will be approaching the time when it is ready to present its recommendations to the client. There will still, however, be several things to be done. Up to this point, the concentration of creative effort will have been on the main items of the campaign – the press layouts, the television scripts (and storyboards or animatic slides or pilot films) and poster designs, whichever is appropriate to the plan. In order to show the creative material in its proper perspective, and also to prove that the strategy is workable in real promotional conditions, most agencies will produce a selection of miscellaneous pieces of creative work which will extend and adapt the central creative theme. These will consist of showcards, dispensers, window stickers, dump bins, mobiles, shelf strips, price tags, or anything else which the agency feels will help to 'merchandise' the campaign at the point of sale, and each tailored to the requirements of the campaign.

Trade Press and Salesmen. Another important element of the campaign will be the support to be given to the client's sales force in the way of trade press advertising, which will give details of the consumer advertising to the retail trade and which will provide a helpful background to the personal selling effort. At the same time, the agency may also feel that it is desirable to design salesmen's 'merchandisers' – visual interpretations of the sales story to be used during the sales interview. (There are widely differing opinions as to the value of these selling aids: some salesmen find them inhibiting and distracting, others derive a great deal of use from them. Their main advantage is that they help to provide a consistent sales presentation and act as a checklist of important points to be covered.)

Sales Promotion. The final element in the creative presentation will be recommendations and suggestions on possible sales promotions. It will usually by now have been decided, either by the client himself or in discussion with the agency, what proportion of the total budget is to be devoted to 'below-the-line' (or non-media) promotion. This will normally be budgeted as a sales, rather than an advertising, cost, but since there is a high degree of creativity involved in devising effective and interesting promotions the agency will often be asked to investigate this area.

Sales promotion takes many forms, and, as in every other aspect of marketing planning, the choice depends entirely on the objectives which need to be achieved. The common objective, of course, is to increase sales of the product, but there are many methods available, some working faster than others; in general, a manufacturer should hope, after a successful promotion, to see his sales level out at a higher point on the graph when the short-term boost of the promotion has died away, thus assuring himself that the promotion has gained either new customers for his product or increased usage of his product amongst existing customers.

The agency will thus need to select the most appropriate type of promotion, having first carefully defined its objectives. To encourage new consumers to buy the product, it will probably recommend some form of sampling operation through the use of coupons or reduced-price offers or banded packs (packing two products together at a price lower than that of the two combined); to stimulate repeat purchases, a longer-term promotion in the form of a competition may be suggested, carrying attractive prizes and requiring the purchase of several units of the product; depending on the type of product involved, a short-term competitive advantage can be achieved through the use of give-away premiums (butter knives, measuring spoons, plastic bowls, etc.), usually associated with the use of the product in some way, or, on a longer-term basis, through the offer of write-in premiums (attractively-priced items obtainable by sending money and packet tops or labels or coupons to the manufacturer himself or to a supplier). Write-in promotions have the extra advantage of providing useful information on the location of response.

The agency's involvement in the creation of these promotions will be two-fold. Firstly, it will investigate and research the opportunities available, particularly for those promotions which require the purchase of other products such as premium items. (There has now grown up a sizeable industry devoted to the production of these items; it even holds a trade fair every year.) This will clearly be the responsibility of the agency's merchandising/sales promotion department.[1] Secondly, the creative department will be required to produce the advertising material necessary to support each promotion: naturally, in these circumstances, it is the promotion itself (the offer, the competition, etc.) which has to be advertised, not the product, since sales of the product will follow automatically if the promotion is successful.

Some promotions, if successful, cost nothing at all, particularly premium offers; these are known as 'self-liquidating' promotions. The principle is that the consumer price of the premium is fixed in such a

[1] See Chapter 6 for a discussion of new developments in this field.

way as to cover its total cost to the manufacturer at a certain projected sales volume level; the consumer price will also cover extra sales and advertising costs, so that any sales above that level will carry not only the normal manufacturing profit but also profit on the premium itself. Not that profit on the sale of premiums is an important promotional objective: manufacturers are content that the promotion should pay for itself.

The Written Plan. Having produced all this material, the agency's preparation for the presentation is almost complete. Only one final, and most important, element is necessary: the agency's recommendation document, setting out in written form the rationale of strategy under every heading, and supporting the argument with statistical media or research data when required. This document is very important for many reasons: firstly, it is a permanent record of the work the agency has done for the campaign; secondly, it obviates many potential arguments when the campaign eventually has to be assessed after the event (hindsight is a particularly strong suit with clients); and thirdly, it allows comparisons to be made between one year and another for the purpose of establishing trends.

Naturally, there are no rigid rules on how to write documents of advertising recommendations; indeed, some agencies leave them unwritten altogether. In principle, they should cover three main areas: firstly, they should analyse the situation; secondly, they should establish objectives; and thirdly, they should set out the strategy.

The situation analysis should contain as much relevant background information as possible. It should survey past advertising performance and relate it to sales results, including if possible any research data on penetration or recall. It should examine sales patterns over the previous year, both of the client's product and competition, in geographical, seasonal and preferably socio-economic terms. It should analyse trends in both above- and below-the-line competitive advertising activity during the previous twelve months from the point of view of weight and content. It should discuss any new research findings which may have a bearing on the current advertising problem, and it should outline any important factors which may influence the preparation of advertising strategy. Finally, of course, it should summarise the terms of reference which have been set for the advertising period under review.

The section dealing with objectives should, after a full discussion of the major problems in each area of activity, clearly set out the targets which any creative, media and promotional strategies will have to achieve. It should treat each of these areas separately, since objectives will inevitably vary in nature for each activity: creative objectives will be largely behavioural and linguistic, media objectives will deal with coverage and frequency targets, and promotional objectives will be very much a matter of sales targets.

The most important section (and certainly the most interesting to the client) will be that on strategy. Here again, each main area of activity will be treated separately. In the case of the media plan, the document will contain a series of tables and charts which will give details of selected publications and television stations, with a breakdown of space sizes, frequency, circulation and readership figures, cumulative coverage, opportunities to see, regional and socio-economic variations and, of course, cost (both physical cost and cost per thousand readers or viewers). These charts will frequently be produced on a large scale also, for the purpose of the presentation itself.

The Presentation. There are many stories about advertising presentations, some funny, some salutary, some perfectly frightening. The care that goes into their planning would sometimes do credit to a theatre producer, so exhaustive are the tactics used. Yet it is not surprising that so much attention is paid to the preparation: the agency has almost certainly spent a great deal of time (and therefore money) on producing what it believes to be the right answers to the problems, and clients are notoriously fickle and sometimes so downright perverse on such occasions, that to have work turned down as a result of tactical errors of presentation can be depressing and frustrating. There was once a cartoon in one of the advertising trade papers which showed a typical tycoon sitting at his desk facing a small, frightened advertising executive. The desk was heaped high with torn-up layouts. The caption read: 'And what's more, Mr Jones, I don't like the colour of your tie!' The joke, though larger than life, aptly illustrates the sort of unpredictable reactions that advertising presentations can stimulate in a way that no other sort of presentation can. It probably stems from the fact that advertising, not being a quantitative science, tempts everybody to become an expert.

Presentations are normally made by the account group, usually the account director, but frequently by an account executive: the choice depends largely on the importance of the client and the ability of the executive himself. Occasionally (again depending on the circumstances) representatives from other departments will be there in support, sometimes even at the client's request, although many clients prefer not to be faced by too many people since it seems to cramp their style. On the other hand, the agency will often find itself faced by a whole army of client executives, ranging from the chairman to the most junior product manager, or, worse still, by the entire client board of directors in their boardroom, most of whom have only a very hazy idea of the business in hand.

Having made its presentation, the agency will have to do one of two things. If the client is happy with the recommendations, the way will be clear to put them into practice. If he is not, the agency will have to go through the whole performance again, and continue to do so until it obtains the client's approval; this may involve devising an entirely new strategy as a result of a fundamental disapproval of principles by the client, but it is much more likely to be a matter of revisions of implementation, either creatively or in media planning.

Campaign Implementation

Ideally, the agency should be in a position to put a campaign into production at least three months before it is due to start, because a lot will need to be done. In particular, there will be three major items.

Media Buying. First, the media plan agreed by the client will have to be booked. This is a highly skilled task, carried out by a media buyer, as distinct from the media planner; most agencies have specialist buyers for press and television, while planners by definition need to look at the media situation as a whole.

Press. In the case of press media buying, the buyer will need to negotiate with the various publications on the schedule for the best days of the week, the best page positions, the most attractive discount rates, the most effective frequency patterns, basing his demands on a battery of readership information from both independent sources and the media owners themselves. Orders will be sent and bookings confirmed. With most press media, there will be little difficulty in obtaining satisfactory space, but there are some publications which may not, especially at short notice, be able to accept orders as a result of excessive demand. The most notorious publications in this category are the women's magazines, particularly the two largest, *Woman* and *Woman's Own*. The reason is not hard to find: the housewife is the most common advertising target – for groceries, toiletries, cosmetics and fashion – and the women's magazines represent the press medium with the minimum wastage of readership for housewife coverage with the added advantage of colour. Therefore, it is advisable to book early.

Television. Television time buying, on the other hand, involves rather different considerations, although of course the principle is the same. Ever since commercial television became a major force in advertising communication, it has commanded a very significant share of total expenditure. Its appearance virtually guaranteed success, since it was the first new addition to available media since commercial radio, and like most innovative developments it did not lack allegiance. Of late the television bubble, while not exactly bursting, has become prodigiously distended, due for the most part to ever-increasing rates and mediocre programme content. The competitive edge it once had over the non-commercial channels has become blunted, and there has been a noticeable drift in viewership figures back to the BBC. The recent re-allocation of area contracts (the most important of which were the amalgamation of the original double London contract – Rediffusion and ATV – into the hands of Thames Television and the unification of the two northern – Lancashire and Yorkshire – stations into one) has done little to redress this balance, and the problems therefore remain. The press is slowly reasserting itself as an advertising medium, and television, despite the advent of the commercial colour channel, is having to fight on very different ground. The latest figures, however, published by the Advertising Association, show that television has, after a fairly static period in the late sixties, picked up again in 1971, as the table opposite indicates.

Thus, while total advertising expenditure has risen each year, showing a growth of almost 30 per cent between 1967 and 1971, the share represented by television has in fact declined by 3 per cent even though there was an increase in the physical amount spent on television in 1971 of almost £20 million. There are also indications that television has

	1967		1968		1969		1970		1971	
	£m	%	£m	%	£m	%	£m	%	£m	%
National newspapers	84	18	99	19	111	20	108	19	108	18
Regional newspapers	108	23	121	23	135	24	143	25	152	25
Magazines/periodicals	46	10	50	10	53	9	51	9	54	9
Trade/technical	43	9	46	9	50	9	53	9	52	9
Other press	7	1	8	2	9	2	11	2	13	2
Production costs	20	4	23	4	29	5	34	6	39	6
TOTAL PRESS	308	65	347	67	387	69	400	70	418	69
Television	124	27	129	25	129	23	125	22	143	23
Poster and outdoor	18	4	20	4	21	4	22	4	23	4
Outdoor signs	15	3	15	3	16	3	17[a]	3	18[a]	3
Cinema	6	1	6	1	6	1	6	1	6	1
Radio	2	—	1	—	1	—	1	—	1	—
	473	100	518	100	560	100	571	100	609	100

[a] BBTA estimates
Source: Advertising Association

Fig. 4 Advertising expenditure by types of media

made further headway since then, for during the first eight months of 1972 television expenditure showed an increase of 25 per cent over the corresponding period in the previous year, against an increase of only 19 per cent in press advertising.

This change of emphasis has had an effect on the problems which face the time buyer. No longer is the choice of television for a popular household product automatic: it has to be judged against the competing attractions and advantages of the press. In the past, his function was in a sense rather mechanical; the relative advantages of peak time and off-peak time were calculated mathematically according to the historical evidence of audience measurement reports; individual programmes created their own particular audience levels; and the effects of the rival attractions of BBC sport or national occasions or the 'official' events were to a large extent predictable. They are no longer: the pattern of viewership has become far more fickle and the function of the time buyer that much more hazardous.

Nevertheless, buying time on television depends for its accuracy and economy on two major considerations – cost and audience size. By varying the balance between high (peak) audience ratings at high cost and low (off-peak) ratings at low cost, the buyer can construct a spot pattern which, evaluated at the end of the campaign, can be proved to have been more economical and effective than any other balance between the two segments. Generally speaking, the best audience for one product on television is the best audience for all products: that is to say, the highest overall audience rating will usually be the highest rating for any specified audience group. Thus, apart from for isolated and highly specialised audiences (such as children), the considerations governing the function of time buying are universal to all products and markets.

As with the popular women's magazines, prime time on television is often scarce and can be obtained only after protracted negotiation: indeed, agencies frequently buy considerable quantities of air-time before even knowing their requirements and subsequently allocate their options to different clients as and when plans are finalised. Of course, the situation has improved in the last year or two with the decline in television's ascendancy.

The major difference between television and the national press lies in the degree of area flexibility. While it is true that it is possible to achieve very broad variations through buying space in specific regional issues of some of the larger national newspapers, the national press is by no means as manœuvrable an instrument as television. With the exception of the television magazines themselves (*Radio Times* and *TV Times*), which are in any case geared to the requirements of area viewing, and local newspapers, which lack the authority and sometimes the immediacy of the national publications, there is nothing to compare with the regionality of the British television network. In this the United Kingdom is almost unique, no other country except Japan being able to offer advertisers a truly national press; it is for this reason that it is difficult to learn many lessons from United States media experience, where the patterns and problems of media planning and buying are on a much more regional scale.

Television in the UK is based on the inherent requirements of specific target consumer groups, both BBC and ITV, and it is the direct competition between the two channels, area by area, which influences the media buyer when he negotiates for client air-time. There are fourteen area stations, varying in size from the large (London, Midlands, Granada, Yorkshire) to the medium (Southern, Tyne Tees, Scottish, Harlech, Westward, Anglia) and the small (Border, Grampian, Ulster and Channel). Each of these regions is controlled by a different contractor, who is responsible for programme content and the organisation of advertising arrangements. His contract is reviewed at the end of its period, and if it is felt by the ITA that there are better claimants to the contract it is allocated elsewhere (as happened in the case of TWW – now Harlech Television – and others after the first review). The relative importance of each station is shown in Fig. 5.

	1968		1970		1971	
	£m	%	£m	%	£m	%
Thames (London Mon.–Fri.)	22·88	15·3	23·15	16·1	27·49	16·4
London Weekend	17·89	12·0	18·53	12·9	21·26	12·8
Midlands ATV	22·21	14·9	21·17	14·7	24·24	14·6
Granada	21·54	14·5	19·08	13·2	23·96	14·4
Yorkshire	13·61	9·1	13·33	9·3	6·61	4·0
STV	9·01	6·0	3·76	2·6	1·87	1·1
Harlech	9·98	6·7	9·93	6·8	10·40	6·3
Southern	10·19	6·8	10·53	7·3	11·66	7·0
Tyne Tees	6·60	4·4	6·11	4·2	3·14	1·9
Anglia	5·89	4·0	6·44	4·5	7·57	4·6
Ulster	2·33	1·6	2·04	1·4	2·35	1·4
Westward	2·78	1·9	2·44	1·7	2·79	1·7
Border	1·29	0·9	1·24	0·9	1·30	0·8
Grampian	2·47	1·7	0·88	0·6	0·19	0·1
STAGS[a]	—	—	5·48	3·8	8·58	5·2
TRIDENT[b]	—	—	—	—	12·75	7·7
	148·67	100	144·11	100	166·16	100

[a] Set up in May 1970 as a combined sales operation for STV and Grampian
[b] Set up in 1971 as a combined sales operation for Yorkshire and Tyne Tees
Source: MEAL, 1971

N.B. The totals differ from those in Fig. 4, due to the fact that MEAL figures are based on gross rate card costs and do not take discounts into consideration.

Fig. 5 Television by contractor 1968–1971 (excluding Channel Islands)

Radio. Media other than press and television are normally regarded as secondary (or support) media. Into this category come radio, outdoor media (posters, bus sides, tube cards, etc.) and the cinema. There are at the moment very few opportunities for radio advertising, since government action effectively put an end to the activities of the 'pirate' stations which operated in the mid-sixties from vessels anchored outside the territorial limits of the UK – Radio Caroline, Radio London and the rest. The only remaining commercial radio frequency receivable in Britain is Radio Luxembourg, and the areas of reception are very patchy (only 28 per cent of the population ever listens to it). Rates tend to be cheap, and the products which are advertised appeal either to young listeners or housewives – the typical 'background music' audiences. Recently, the development of the BBC's Radio One has taken toll of this audience. Few, if any products, can afford to depend entirely on Radio Luxembourg for their advertising support since (*a*) audience coverage is limited, and (*b*) there is no visual product association. Time is bought on a 'block' basis (so many spots of a given length per night or day over a given period).

A government White Paper (March 1971) proposed to allow private firms to set up some sixty urban commercial radio stations in competition with the BBC. The first (LBC) opened in 1973, and the ITA (renamed the IBA) administers the system. It will be very interesting to see how this will affect the pattern of media expenditure.

Outdoor. Outdoor advertising is at last beginning to emerge from its period in the wilderness as an unquantifiable hit-or-miss operation, and attempts are now being made to put its deployment on a more scientifically costable basis. The use of techniques such as devices for measuring the dilation of the pupils of the eyes of passers-by goes some way towards supplying advertisers and agencies with data which can help them evaluate the economics of the medium; but it is doubtful whether outdoor audience measurement will ever reach the degree of sophistication which exists for other media. The result is that outdoor advertising displays are bought to give 'back-up' support to press and television campaigns (again on a 'block' basis of so many sites of a certain standard, usually for not less than thirteen weeks; there are several contractors who lease and service these sites for advertisers, in addition to the transport owners such as British Rail, London Transport and the various bus companies). Because of this, outdoor (particularly poster) sites tend to be used for only a limited number of product groups or services: food, tobacco, petrol, alcoholic drinks and investment are the staple diet of the poster contractors, the reason being that it is possible in these cases to present a very simple message very quickly (it is usually held that people looking at a poster can assimilate a maximum of about seven words at a glance), although it is remarkable how frequently one can find very inappropriate uses of the medium.

Cinema. Finally, the cinema: this has been left until last since in many ways it is the most interesting of all media, not least of all because of its application to so many different situations and its constantly changing role in the total advertising picture. Until the availability of commercial television, the cinema presented the sole opportunity for advertising in movement (and consequently the chance to demonstrate products in use); what is more, it allowed this to be done in colour.

The television age affected the cinema in two ways. Firstly, audiences were drawn away from the large to the small screen, and the whole pattern of leisure time changed virtually overnight; many cinemas closed or became bingo halls; a visit to the cinema came to be regarded more as a special occasion than a common event, while the early figures for television viewership showed an alarming number of hours spent in front of the set (an average of five hours a day, seven days a week).

Secondly, the advent of a commercial television channel dealt another blow to the cinema owners: in addition to seeing their audiences dwindling away they now had to suffer the pain of losing substantial amounts of advertising revenue to the new medium. It was a vicious circle, and the cinema took a long time to recover.

Despite these setbacks, however, the cinema has of late recovered some of the ground it lost; this has been achieved largely through changes in film-making policy and a general improvement in standards. Audiences have increased, and consequently so has advertising revenue.

The cinema still has, for advertisers, one major advantage over television: it is very much a young person's medium (70 per cent of regular cinema-goers are under the age of thirty) and thus it can offer a highly competitive alternative for reaching markets which consist essentially of teenagers or twenty- to thirty-year-olds. This is not only more difficult with television (as we have seen, it is less discriminating in its audience coverage), but it is also, as a result, more expensive because of the wastage involved.

One final question still remains to be resolved as far as the cinema is concerned, and that is the effect that colour television will have. Until colour television was available, the cinema had the advantage of being able to feature in high-quality colour what television could only show in black and white. Ownership of colour television sets is still relatively small, and many advertisers continue to produce commercials in black and white, so that it remains to be seen whether cinema advertising revenue will suffer. Nevertheless, the cinema does seem to have rescued itself from what, in the early days of television, appeared to be a hopeless situation.

Cinema screen-time is comparatively cheap, but this is offset by the high cost of film (at least one print has to be made for each cinema used – sometimes hundreds – compared with the one or two copies required by a television contractor); it is not uncommon for films to cost more than screen-time. Cinemas are booked on a number of bases – size, area and type – and can be used for any length of time. Films (of up to two minutes) or slides can be used in special advertising features, and longer films featured separately. Virtually all are in colour.

Press Production. The second major item to be attended to in the process of putting an advertising campaign into effect will be the production of creative material in a form in which it can be used in the press, on the television or cinema screen, on the hoardings or elsewhere.

Press advertisements (it may appear to the layman seeing a highly-finished presentation layout for the first time) need little further attention before sending them off to the newspaper. This is by no means the case; the layout is a substitute for the real thing, and much will need to be done in order to produce the final 'artwork'. The illustration (if there is one) on the layout will usually be one of three things – an artist's impression, a 'stock' (or library) photograph, or a rough photograph taken purely for the purpose of the layout without any thought of further reproduction. When the layouts which constitute the campaign have been approved, however, and preparations are being made for their insertion into press publications, new photography will be necessary in order to provide photographs which, while preserving the atmosphere and purpose of the originals, will satisfy reproduction requirements and be of a much higher quality. Such photographic sessions can be (and frequently are) very expensive, using as they do the very best photographers and models and often involving the purchase, rental or manufacture of elaborate and costly props.

In the preparation of this photography, attention will be paid to such details as tone and key, since publications differ greatly in the clarity of their reproduction. National and provincial newspapers, printed at great speed on low-quality newsprint, are usually produced by the letterpress process, which involves the transfer of ink from a raised surface (a piece of type or the dot in a photograph) to the paper; so are many smaller-circulation publications, but on much higher quality paper. The latter will clearly allow for higher definition and crisper reproduction, so that more subtle effects can be aimed at in the preparation of photographic material. The difference between low- and high-quality letterpress reproduction is usually expressed by screen size (representing the number of dots produced over a linear inch); thus, newspapers are normally printed 55 or 65 screen, while some glossy magazines will be in the region of 130 to 150 screen. Exactly the same considerations will apply to colour letterpress reproduction, except that in this case four or more separate printings, each with different coloured dots, will be carried out, with the additional problem of colour separation. Many photographs will be taken, and a final choice made from several final prints. The chosen photograph will be mounted, cropped, masked and almost certainly retouched before it is ready for the next stage.

Of course, in the case of a graphic (as distinct from a photographic) illustration, the problems are fewer, since the artist will have been carefully briefed to produce exactly the required work, both from an artistic and a reproduction point of view.

The other important element in the preparation of press artwork is typography. Traditionally an art in itself, it can often make a poor advertisement look better than it is, or a good one look exceptional. Some of the basic decisions will already have been taken at the layout stage (the headline, subheads, etc.), but the bulk of the typographical work – the disposition of the columns, etc. – will not be done until artwork is required. A good typographer will base his decisions on the atmosphere of an advertisement and its basic objectives, and will choose from a multitude of typographical possibilities (there are something like 6,000 typefaces, not counting 'home-made' varieties; most have italic forms as well, and some have both an extended and condensed in addition to a light, medium and bold version).

Having decided on his choice of typefaces, and the size and arrangement of copy, the typographer will produce his type 'mark-up'. This will be a tracing of the main elements of the layout, showing the position of illustrations, headlines, brand names or logotypes (the standard description for a brand or company name in a particular house-style) and the area to be occupied by the body copy. He will indicate his instructions as to typeface, size (6-point, 8-point, 12-point, etc.) and number of lines, and he will pencil in the line-endings so that the typesetter will be able to see at which point he is to begin a new line. This mark-up, along with artwork for the illustrations and any other special requirements (such as a diagram or a brand name) will then be sent to the blockmaker for proofing.

The blockmaker, in turn, will do two things. He will make blocks from the assorted pieces of artwork supplied ('line' blocks from graphic work and screen blocks from photographic or tone work according to the screen size specified). This is done by reproducing the artwork photographically on to sensitised metal (the screen is obtained by shooting photographs through a dotted camera mask), coating the image with acid-resistant ink and immersing the metal into an acid bath for a short time, after which the image (lines or dots) is left proud. He will also set the type according to the typographer's instructions.

The two will then be combined into a 'forme' in their proper positions, and the first proofs pulled off and submitted to the agency. The agency will check these, make the necessary corrections and ask the blockmaker either to proceed to the final foundry stage or to submit further proofs. In the foundry, the blockmaker will produce a single metal block from a plastic matrix pressed off the forme and send it, mounted on wood or unmounted, to the publication with the agency's delivery slip. The publication will incorporate this block into its own relevant page forme and from it make its semi-circular metal plates which are clamped to the rollers of the press. Fortunately, after these many stages and frequent reversals of image, the advertisement appears the correct way round in the publication.

A word should be said at this point about artwork for advertisements which are destined for reproduction in publications produced by processes other than letterpress. These fall into two categories, gravure and photolithography: while they call for virtually the same type of artwork, they are quite different printing processes, even though the difference between the results is sometimes difficult to distinguish. Gravure simply reverses the letterpress technique: the raised parts of the printing plate are wiped clean of ink, and the paper is printed from the ink left in the depressions; the effect is softer than letterpress, and the process is by far the cheapest of the three for very long print runs. Lithography (which takes its name from the original flat stone plates used in its early days) involves the imposition of a photographic image on a sensitised metal roller; the image is water-repellent but the rest of the roller's surface is not. The roller is wetted, and afterwards the image is inked with a greasy ink which is repelled by the wet areas, thus ensuring that only the image is printed. This process is used for the highest standard of reproduction and can produce magnificent effects. A variation is offset lithography, where the ink is transferred from the metal roller to a rubber roller by which the paper is printed (the image in this case is of course double-reversed). Offset litho is now becoming increasingly common for some small newspapers.

Since no blocks (such as those used in letterpress printing) are required for gravure or lithography, the material which will be sent to the publication by the agency is the artwork itself. This will be a complete image of the advertisement, with all the elements correctly positioned and every word of copy printed and pasted down; such printed type (called 'repro') is obtained from a blockmaking and typesetting house by the typographer in exactly the same way that he will obtain the proof of a letterpress advertisement. In the case of colour artwork, illustrations will consist either of colour transparencies or dye-transfers (very accurate and expensive colour prints produced from transparencies). One of the difficulties with gravure publications (lithography is used more for miscellaneous material such as leaflets, brochures and mail-order catalogues) is that it is impossible to make alterations once the publication has made its plates; great accuracy and high quality are therefore essential in artwork produced for this purpose.

The timing of all this activity is, of course, critical. In the case of newspaper (letterpress) advertisements, blocks can be produced virtually overnight, providing that artwork is available, but such rapid production is generally undesirable, especially at the beginning of a new campaign: it leaves no time for correction and the final result is likely to be poor; it also finds very little favour with blockmakers. Normally, several days will be allowed, so that the chances of error can be minimised and better quality assured.

The responsibility for programming art and production work is finally in the hands of the account group, who have to ensure that the advertisement will appear as planned, and have to obtain client approval at every stage, but the immediate operational function will be supervised by the art director appointed to the specific account. He is the person who decides on the original artistic treatment (photography, drawings, etc.) and consequently the one who chooses the photographer, models, location, artist and all the other factors influencing the preparation of artwork; he will also select the best print or drawing and decide on the amount of retouching; and finally he will liaise very closely with the production department (responsible for putting in hand all typesetting and blockmaking) so as to ensure that his artwork gets the best possible treatment (in the case of gravure printing, of course, he can do little after the artwork has been released to the publisher except keep in the closest contact with the publisher's own production people). The time required for the entire process from approval of creative recommendations to completion of artwork can vary, depending on the complexity of the work, but it will be more a matter of weeks than days.

Similar considerations and procedures will be involved in any other form of print advertising, notably posters, and the length of the art and production schedules will again obviously depend on the type and difficulty of the work concerned.

Television Production. Television production, on the other hand, is a very different matter. We have seen earlier that television creative recommendations can take many forms – scripts, storyboards, animatics (a series of slides with a taped commentary), pilot films, etc. – but, unlike press layouts, these recommendations can never really hope to represent as close an indication of the final article as is in principle desirable, largely because of the difficulties involved in maintaining a high standard of filming over a sustained length of time. Still photography can, perhaps deliberately or accidentally, capture in one out of many shots just the impression the creative team is aiming for, but with moving film the chances are much more slim.

In a sense, therefore, it is not until he sees the results of the final professional shooting sessions that a client can be certain that he approves of the agency's work. Thus he can decide, at the agency's presentation, only in principle on the ideas he receives, and the agency will frequently have to defend those ideas, and obtain approval of them, by persuading the client to accept on trust that the film technique will communicate them successfully. Some agency men would disagree that such trust is ever necessary. (Brian Palmer of KMPH wrote in *The Financial Times* in August 1971 that if an idea could not stand on its own merits, no amount of dependence on technique could improve it; this is, of course, true in principle, but few clients are capable of judging anything but the final implementation of a creative idea. I once had a client who blankly refused to make his approval of creative work final until he saw it in the pages of the press or on his television screen.) Nevertheless, client approval will be necessary at every stage of television production, as in all other agency activity.

Television production is a very specialised business, and the agency will usually have a department specifically responsible for it; but while, as in the case of press production, the agency's creative team will maintain very close contact with the progress of the production of a film, the onus of decision will be very firmly in the hands of the television producer. The producer will be responsible for selecting the production company (no agency can economically make its own films) on the basis of a balance of cost and suitability. Some production companies build up a reputation of excellence in specific areas (food, unusual effects, location shots, etc.) and the producer will, when comparing quotations received from different companies, have to consider whether a difference in cost represents a corresponding difference in quality; thus it is not always the cheapest quotation which is accepted.

The producer may well select a production company because he wants a particular director to make his film. In any event, once the quotation has been accepted, the first step will be to select a film crew (cameraman, lighting, etc.) and to draw up a production schedule and shooting script. In the meantime, work will begin on set design and model selection.

The shooting script is the result of a pre-production meeting at which all the details of the production are worked out in such a way as to eliminate the maximum number of problems during the shooting of the film. The director will, at this meeting, make suggestions which, while not changing significantly any elements of the script or storyboard itself, can or should improve or increase the effectiveness of the film's communication of its message.

It may well also be necessary, before the actual shooting begins, to carry out film tests on specific aspects of the film such as details of the set, or shots of the pack or product, or facial expressions. Frequently (especially with pack shot tests) this will be done on closed-circuit television in the agency.

The production schedule will begin with the pre-production meeting and will finish with the dispatch of final prints to the different programme contractors. The shooting date (or dates) will be fixed so as to enable all preparatory work to be carried out in time (casting, construction of sets, selection of location(s), hiring of crew, organising supplies of product, arranging cooking facilities for food photography, and so on), and shooting can take anything up to four or five days to complete, especially on location abroad. This may sound excessive for the filming of a few seconds of screen-time, but it must be remembered that commercials are on a much more concentrated scale than feature films, where longer continuous sequences (sometimes of several minutes' duration) are involved; in a 30-second commercial there can be as many as half a dozen different sequences, all requiring careful setting up.

After the completion of filming, the first visible results will be the 'rushes' (rough prints of all the material shot at each session). From these (there will be prints of several takes of each sequence) the director and producer will select the best on the basis of individual quality and total film continuity. These will then be edited into a complete reel or 'rough cut', and at this stage the film will have neither sound nor titling (opticals). The client may be called to view the film at this stage, but is not normally.

At the same time the sound track will be recorded separately (artists having previously been chosen and music written); it is frequently necessary to dub voices, in which case the recording will be made with the film running to ensure synchronisation. Sometimes, of course, film will be shot and voices recorded simultaneously, but this is less common.

An edited sound track of voices, music and other sound effects will then be produced, and the film and track synchronised but not yet married together. They are thus ready for showing in 'double head' form, which requires a special projector into which both tape and soundtrack are fed and run through in perfect synchronisation, giving the effect of a normal sound film. Again, the opticals are still missing, but the client will normally at this stage be asked to come and approve the film since it is the last stage at which corrections can be made before production is complete.

The corrections that can be made, however, are very limited. Short of reshooting the film, either in part or entirely, they are restricted to changes of key or tone of print, the substitution of alternative takes, rerecording of track or changes in editing. These limitations illustrate

1 The most famous of all Bovril advertisements, 1896.

2 Bovril advertisement, 1890. Impossible today.

3 The Pears Lillie Langtry advertisement, with the signature that lost her £40,000.

4 Sunlight Soap advertisement, 1888. Good motivational stuff.

5 Ovaltine advertisement, 1922. Hearts and flowers.

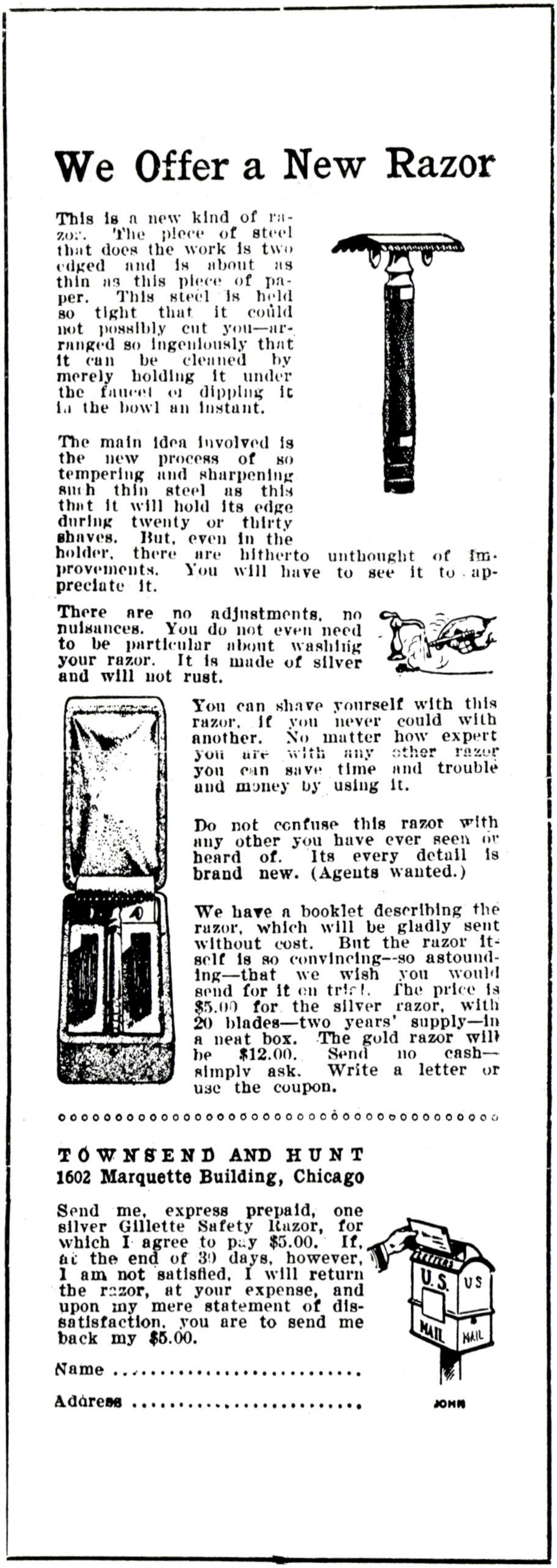

6 The first Gillette advertisement (US), 1903. A classic example of strong, readable copy.

7 Guinness advertisement, 1952. Advertising humour at its best.

8 Cadbury's Drinking Chocolate advertisement, 1965. Perfect harmony between product, visual and headline.

9 Typical advertising layout, and the advertisement produced from it.

SHINNERS · HIGH STREET · SUTTON · Phone 01-642 6000
SHINNERS
OUR BUYERS FINAL SALE REDUCTIONS
SAVE UP TO 50% ON PERFECT PRICE
TEMPLETONS WILTON
12" TWIST PILE BROADLOOM
Excellent for general domestic use, in Red, Brown, Green, Off white, Gold or dark Green.
Reorder Price £3.99sqyd
£2.99 SQ YD
HALF PERFECT PRICE CARPETS
LUXURY VELVET PILE GLENDONALD
100% Pure wool pile, 27" wide
Reorder price When perfect £6.95 yd
£3.45 YD
& 15' wide
Tremendous value
Reorder price When perfect £7.75
£5.50 SQ YD
BROAD KINKY TWIST PILE 18' & 9' wide
Reorder price When perfect £7.65
£4.99 SQ YD
SAVE OVER £16
8' BEDROOM FITMENTS
from Britain's largest Manufacturer comprises Superb louvered door fronts in a white natural finish—Hanging robe, Fitted robe, Dressing Table Unit and 3 large Top Cupboards
List price £164.50
£148
EASI-BUY 1.72 weekly 2 yrs to pay
THIRD OFF TODAYS VALUE FURNITURE
SAVE 1/3 TODAY'S VALUE
'LIMELIGHT'
3 drawer chests with smart 'Tola' finish
TODAYS VALUE £26.44
£16.95
SAVE 1/3 TODAYS VALUE
'DURABLE'
3'9" Hanging Wardrobe
Pine/White Finish
TODAYS VALUE £54.10
£35.95
EASI-BUY 76p weekly 1 year to pay
2'10" Fitted Wardrobe. Pine white.
TODAYS VALUE £48.20
£31.95
EASI-BUY 68p weekly 1 year to pay
SAVE UP TO £36 TV & AUDIO
ONKYO SM10
Stereo System superb Value with ★ 12" turntable ★ 20W music power ★ VHF Stereo radio plus MW.
Rec price £126.30
£89.95
EASI-BUY £1.04 weekly 2 yrs to pay
WITH FREE HEADPHONES WORTH £3.75
HITACHI
This Fabulous 18" colour TV has outstanding guarantees Finished in Smart Teak.
Rec price £235
£214.95
SAVE £20
EASI-BUY £1.79 weekly 3 yrs to pay
HALF TODAYS VALUE SOFT FURNISHINGS
by JAMES TODD
LIGHTWEIGHT ACRYLIC WEAVE
48" wide - in Yellow, Green, Red, Orange
Todays Value £1.59
79p YD
1/2 TODAY'S VALUE
AMERICAN DUPION 'TAJ MAHAL'
48" in White, Citrus, Lilac, Gold
Todays Value £2.29
99p YD
OSMAN
PRINTED SATIN 48"
Superb floral design in Turquoise, Green & Dove Grey
Todays Value £1.79
89p YD
1/2 TODAYS VALUE
FASHION SAVINGS UP TO & OVER £5
'QUELRAYN' 'SIMON BLAIR AND '4 SEASONS' Showerproofs
a superb Selection
ALL AT £9.99
FOR EXAMPLE
'QUELRAYN' SEE PICTURE
A smart little shower-proof at a good saving
usually £15.50
£9.99
SAVE OVER £5
SAVE £2
CHECKED HOSTESS DRESSES
Special purchase Value £6.99
£4.99
WOOL SHOP IN THE ARCADE
ALMOST 1/2 PRICE
Bairnswear
Machinewashable Tricel/Nylon 4 ply double knit ideal for knitting & crochet
Usually 15p
8p 25 gms

10 Typical advertising layout, and the advertisement produced from it.

very forcibly the responsibility which lies on the agency to produce satisfactory material. In the event of a complete or part reshoot being necessary, the cost will almost certainly have to be borne jointly by production company and agency, unless a clause specifically providing for such an eventuality has been written into the production agreement.

If the film is approved, the opticals (any graphic work – usually lettering) are drawn and a married print consisting of film, sound track and opticals produced, from which bulk prints are made to be sent to the programme contractors. These are normally costed into the initial production costs, although subsequent artists' repeat fees (a royalty on each transmission) are not.

Mention should be made here of a technique which is becoming increasingly popular for short campaigns or immediate transmissions (such as the announcement of a new price following a tax cut, or a petrol advertisement using topical material such as a Grand Prix victory the previous day). Clearly, in cases such as this there is no time to go through the protracted production programme described above, so some alternative has to be found. This is the video-tape or VTR (video telerecording) commercial, filmed in exactly the same way as that in which the television companies themselves record programmes for repeat transmission. Its advantage is speed of production, but it also costs very little (a fraction of a proper production); its disadvantages are poorer quality (as might be expected in such a rushed piece of work) and the fact that there is a limit on the number of times it can be screened (although it rarely happens that it is produced for anything other than a very limited series of transmissions).

One constraint which applies to television advertising alone, and which influences every stage of the writing and production of commercials, is the need to satisfy the copy clearance department of the ITCA (Independent Television Companies Association). All scripts must be submitted for clearance before production, which means, of course, that there is little point in showing scripts to the client before the ITCA's approval has been obtained. Furthermore, no film can be transmitted before it has been seen and approved by the ITCA as a true version of the script.

The ITCA's regulations are strict, and in some cases curiously self-contradictory. For instance, cigarette advertising is forbidden on television because of the dangers to health, but at the same time many charitable institutions which advertise to raise funds for the treatment and cure of, or research into, diseases such as cancer are also banned. Some of the ITCA's rulings on individual scripts are similarly difficult to understand: nuances of interpretation of words, phrases or situations are sometimes magnified out of all proportion, and the tortuous arguments which are advanced to show that viewers could be misled or corrupted frequently baffle even the agencies themselves.

Nevertheless, the ITCA does ensure safety, even if it sometimes inhibits creative imagination. There is no doubt that television is better for it, and in many ways it is regrettable that the vetting mechanisms of other media do not impose such stringent requirements.

Cinema Production. Cinema production follows very much the same lines as television, but without the need to pay attention to the constraints of copy supervision. The cinema, of course, has offered the opportunity for colour advertising for a long time, and few cinema commercials are made in black and white. Traditionally, the main difference between filming commercials for the cinema and television has been one of lead time: colour presents its own problems and processing takes longer; but now this difference has disappeared and, although most television sets still show everything in monochrome, most commercials are made in colour. The difference in production cost between the cinema and television lies in the cost of prints, many more of which are required for a cinema campaign.

Radio Production. Radio production is the last to be discussed, partly because it is the least complicated, but more particularly because radio advertising is less common in Britain than in some other parts of the world (notably the USA) and certainly less important than any other medium. Writing for the radio (commercially, that is) is not the highly specialised operation that television writing is; in many ways, it is very little different from writing for the press. As we have seen, after the disappearance of the pirate radio stations, only one commercial radio station (Radio Luxembourg) was receivable in the UK, but it is interesting to speculate what effect local commercial radio will nowhave on other media, particularly the local and regional press.

In the US, the sponsored television or radio programme is a common occurrence. In Britain, both television and radio advertising activity is based on the 'commercial break' principle, so that there are few opportunities, when writing campaigns for radio, to be imaginative. Television offers much greater possibilities through being a visual medium. All, therefore, that is required for radio production is an effective presenter and a good recording. The recording is quickly rehearsed, taped, edited and released.

Miscellaneous Production. It goes almost without saying that, in addition to the production of material for appearance in different media, the agency will at the same time be preparing the miscellaneous material required for campaign support – the many items of literature such as brochures, display units, promotional pieces (coupons, special labels, etc.), salesmen's merchandisers and the like. In many cases, artwork used for press advertising can be used for these items as well, and the processes of production are very similar. The client will require estimates for printing; indeed, he will often elect to get such items printed himself, since it is difficult for agencies to be competitive when they are adding their own commission to printers' quotations.

Co-ordination of Effort. The third important element in campaign preparation is less concerned with technique; it serves a different, but critically important, purpose – co-ordination of human effort.

One of the fundamental, but unfortunately too seldom observed, principles of advertising strategy (indeed, one which frequently makes the difference between success and failure) is that, at all points of contact between company and customer, the communicated image should be consistently the same. There are many such contacts: mass communication (advertising and public relations), the product (packaging), personal relationships (salesmen, service staff, information departments) as well as the multifarious executive activities which bring company personnel face to face with members of the public and of other commercial and industrial organisations. Too often I have seen a fine advertising campaign blunted because it has not received the support of other activities.

A few years ago a major British charity (one of the oldest established in its field) recognised the need to position itself more positively in the context of the many more recently founded charities. Its image was old-fashioned, and, since the social problems which it had been originally set up to alleviate had either totally disappeared or changed out of all recognition, the public found it difficult to identify its purpose with the conditions prevailing in modern Britain; what is more, the public tended to feel that, since the activity of the organisation was a domestic (as distinct from an overseas) activity, it was merely duplicating the efforts of the welfare state. The problem was clearly an enormous one, for although the charity was genuinely fulfilling a necessary role it was attempting to prove the fact in the face of very firmly rooted public misconception. The agency handling the account devised an excellent campaign strategy, and produced some highly effective advertising based on this strategy; the campaign's strength lay in its overall image – building an identity which could be illustrated across every item of printed literature, every collecting box and every flag-day lapel sticker. Unfortunately, while all this was accepted with enthusiasm by the appeals staff, it was never given the chance to percolate to the operational staff, with the result that the image was diffused, fragmented and less effective. It was only with some difficulty that the following year the conflict was resolved and the campaign given a proper chance: it has now achieved its purpose.

The example has not been taken from a typical commercial environment, but it serves very well to illustrate the importance of the point at issue: that every member of the client's organisation should be fully aware of and conversant with the objectives and content of the publicity effort.

The major task confronting the agency in this context will be to prepare the client's sales team for the approaching campaign. For this purpose a sales conference is essential: in co-operation with sales management, the agency must present the advertising plan to the sales force; it must fully explain its creative strategy, product by product; it must give salesmen details of media support, with schedules of timing, sizes, spot length, publications and television stations used; it must supply them with pulls of advertisements and television storyboards; it must give them examples of all merchandising support items; and by explaining the evidence for adopting such a strategy (research surveys, sales audit data, advertisement tests) it must equip them with the ammunition for their selling effort. The agency must also show how individual sales areas will benefit from the campaign (extra support for area weakness or greater sales potential); and finally it must present the promotional plan in all its aspects (competitions, special offers, trade deals, area promotions) and indicate how the sales force can best implement this plan to its own advantage (salesmen's incentive schemes). The agency will, throughout the conference, work closely with client sales and marketing executives to ensure the greatest level of support and enthusiasm from the sales force, and to guarantee maximum smoothness of operation once the campaign is under way.

In organisations where there is no travelling sales force (such as, for example, a chain of retail stores or a bank or British Rail), a conference of key executives – branch managers or regional managers – will still be necessary for the proper co-ordination of activity and attitudes. The consumer must be presented with a consistent image.

Campaign Control

We have seen how an advertising campaign is created and produced. It might be thought that the agency's function is now complete; in reality, however, this is just where the routine of advertising agency operation begins.

The account group (or, in this case, the account executive) will be responsible, while a campaign is running, for three important day-to-day functions: they are schedule rotation, quality control and budget control. These are the fundamental requirements of campaign supervision.

Schedule Rotation. An advertising campaign will usually consist of more than one advertisement; the typical campaign will be a series of variations on a central theme, using different headlines, situations, and scripts. In addition, there may well be different sizes of press advertisements, different lengths of television commercials and almost certainly a variety of newspapers, magazines and television stations on the schedule. The more complex the media pattern and the greater the variety of creative material, the more likely it is that mistakes will be made, and it is the good account executive who makes sure that they are not.

At the beginning of a campaign, therefore, the executive will prepare (and agree with his client) a detailed rotation schedule, which will indicate which advertisement or commercial is to be used for each insertion or transmission. Every advertisement and commercial will be given its own reference number; the production department, whose responsibility it is to issue instructions to blockmakers for the dispatch of material to the press, and the television production department, which arranges for television prints to be sent to contractors, will each hold a copy of the rotation schedule and follow the instructions on it. In this way errors should not occur. The rotation schedule can be a very complicated affair, since it will sometimes have to take into account (as has been indicated) a multiplicity of variations of size and type of advertisement, and any extra spaces or spots booked during the course of the campaign will of course be added to it as they occur.

It may be that not all advertisements of a campaign go into production at the same time; it frequently happens that only the first one or two (the ones required to fill insertions for perhaps a month) are prepared in their publishable form before the campaign starts. The reason for this is that there is no sense in overloading art and production departments before the work is really necessary, especially as there will inevitably be demands made on those departments by other accounts simultaneously. The good account executive is the man who can plan his production requirements to suit his schedule requirements and allow adequate time for everything to be completed satisfactorily. This naturally does not apply to television, where considerable savings are effected through shooting a series of commercials at the same time.

Quality Control. As well as supervising the rotation of advertisements along the lines of his planned schedule, the account executive will also be responsible to his client and his account director for the quality of press and television reproduction, for the positions advertisements are given in newspapers or magazines, for the particular times within booked television segments at which his commercials appear, and for generally ensuring that there are no grounds for complaint on any score.

The observation of this responsibility will take two forms, which are best described as pre- and post-control. Pre-control will involve taking every possible precaution to make sure that correct instructions have been issued to press or television media when bookings have been made, and that the material supplied to these media is as good as it possibly can be. The executive needs to have expert reassurance that blocks and plates supplied by the agency are not likely to cause undue problems when they are printed, such as over-inking or liability to suffer from show-through (the term used when an advertisement shows the reverse image of heavily printed matter on the other side of the paper); he also needs to know that television prints produced for transmission are properly graded so that they will screen satisfactorily within the tolerable limits of reception. Finally, he needs, through his media department, to maintain pressure on media owners so that his clients get a fair deal; for example, when press advertisements are booked 'run-of-paper' (i.e. no premium price is paid for a special position), he must try to prevent in advance an uninterrupted succession of bad positions. In short, he needs to ensure that if anything does in the event go wrong it will be the fault of the media themselves and not the agency, and that the agency will thus have legitimate grounds for complaint.

Post-control consists of a careful examination of advertisements after they have appeared or, in the case of television, while they are appearing. He would, for instance, be justified in objecting if his commercial for frozen peas appeared during the same break as a commercial for canned peas, or if an insensitive contractor screened his commercial for sea-cruise holidays in the middle of a documentary about maritime disasters. As for the press, he should certainly complain about poor reproduction (incidentally, bad reproduction, if the block is satisfactory, rarely runs through all copies of an edition, but such copies have a habit of falling into clients' hands) or unsatisfactory positions, providing that the causes cannot be traced to the agency. He will automatically be sent a voucher copy of the publication containing the advertisement, which he must check carefully before it is sent to the client with the invoice. The usual compensation, if the media owner admits liability, is a free insertion or transmission. The important thing, however, is that the executive should take the matter up with the publication or television station responsible *before* the client has the chance to complain himself.

Budget Control. The final, and perhaps most important, element in campaign control is the supervision of the client's budget. This will require close liaison between the account group, the agency's accounts department and the client. No proper control of the deployment of the budget can be possible unless comparison can be made between planned and actual expenditure, at any point in the year and under any budget heading. While the agency clearly has an obligation to be able to do this for its clients, it is also a vital element in the agency's own internal financial control. We saw earlier that most agencies use the borrowing facilities of the banks to ease their cash flow problems; the aggregate of the agency's clients' budgetary plans thus provides the basis for estimating the year's borrowing requirements and profit forecasts.

As Fig. 6 shows, the principle on which advertising budget control is maintained is the correlation of campaign plan figures and actual 'invoiced' amounts. The invoice, of course, will not be paid by the client until some time during the following month, and furthermore will not contain items such as advertisements appearing during the last few days of the month it represents, so that the executive's monthly figures will not correspond exactly with those of either the accounts department or his client: the executive uses the figures for the purpose of ensuring that the budget is not exceeded, and the accounts department as a record of turnover. The client will use them for both.

Financial Systems

It is not out of place to show here how an agency's accounting system works. All expenditure on behalf of clients, whether in the area of media bookings, artwork, production, print or ancillary services such as research, direct mail or sales promotion, will be authorised by an official order from the agency, approval from the client having first been obtained for the purchase. Bills from suppliers will come direct to the agency (not the client); media bills will appear very promptly after the appearance of the advertisement – in fact, some media owners are now so concerned at the delays they experience in payment of their invoices that they are insisting on time penalties of scaled interest for late remittances. Bills from other suppliers will take rather longer: in the case of production charges, where many different advertisements, over a number of weeks, are involved in a particular production exercise, bills may not appear for months.

As invoices are received, it will be the responsibility of the account group to pass them for payment and to allocate to them the proper advertisement reference. Normally, media charges will be passed on to clients immediately (that is, at the end of the month during which they are received); production and art charges are usually held until all the invoices relevant to the production of a given advertisement are to hand

BUDGET CONTROL RECORD

Client ____________________ Period ____________________

Budget £ ____________
Revision 1 £ ____________
Revision 2 £ ____________

MONTH												TOTAL	Anticipated expenditure next 12 months
PLAN Press													
TV													
Outdoor													
Print													
Production													
Other													
TOTAL													
CUMULATIVE TOTAL													
ACTUAL Press													
TV													
Outdoor													
Print													
Production													
Other													
TOTAL													
CUMULATIVE TOTAL													
THIS MONTH OVER/UNDERSPENT													
CUMULATIVE OVER/UNDERSPENT													

Fig. 6 A typical agency budget control sheet

(this obviates the necessity of sending clients supplementary invoices and avoids the possibility of complaints).

The agency, according to the regulations of its governing body (the Institute of Practitioners in Advertising), makes a gross profit of 15 per cent on its transactions (or 17·65 per cent, depending on whether the profit is regarded as being 15 per cent of the gross or net figure – 100 per cent or 115 per cent). In the case of media charges, each publication or television contractor will offer to agencies an official commission rate: with national and most regional media the rate is 15 per cent, but with some trade and special interest media it is 12½ per cent and sometimes even only 10 per cent. In the event of the quoted commission rate being less than 15 per cent, the agency will add the extra 2½ per cent or 5 per cent to bring it up to the standard level. At the same time, it will also adjust the quoted 15 per cent commission to 17·65 per cent of the gross figure. Thus, the following financial calculations are necessary by the agency's accounts department in specific cases of an expenditure of £100:

Medium 1 – quoted commission 15%

Charge to agency £100 less 15%	= £85	
Charge to client £85 plus 17·65%	= £100	
		Profit = £15

Medium 2 – quoted commission 12½%:

Charge to agency £100 less 12½%	= £87·50	
Charge to client £100 less 12½%+17·65%	= £102·94	
		Profit = £15·44

Medium 3 – quoted commission 10%:

Charge to agency £100 less 10%	= £90	
Charge to client £100 less 10%+17·65%	= £105·88	
		Profit = £15·88

It can be seen that, the lower the quoted commission, the greater the marginal benefit to the agency, but it must be remembered that the proportion of total media expenditure accounted for by publications offering less than 15 per cent commission is minimal, and more and more such publications are changing to the 15 per cent rate.

For items other than media charges, the system is more flexible, though there are clearly limits on the amount of profit the agency can make. With suppliers whose services are called upon regularly, such as blockmakers, typesetters and artwork companies, there is normally a standing arrangement on rates (or, for a particularly large or complicated piece of work, a fee is agreed in advance). To these charges, the agency will apply its usual commission. In the case of television production or research services of any kind, the cost is agreed in advance by the agency and its client, and this will include the agency's profit.

Most clients – certainly those who are required to report on their activity to a parent or holding company – insist on receiving copies of suppliers' invoices when they are billed by the agency. This serves two purposes: it clarifies details which may not be immediately obvious from the agency's covering statement; and it ensures that the agency maintains a fair and honest attitude. As in every other business, there is in advertising an element which is not averse to overcharging, although it is the exception rather than the rule.

The commission system contains some obvious anomalies and shortcomings, which will be examined in detail in a later chapter. It is enough to point out here that there is currently a strong movement of opinion in the industry towards a totally different basis of revenue on the principle of negotiated fees. Under this arrangement, all media commissions are rebated to clients and replaced by a fee which is held to represent more realistically the amount of work involved. It is particularly popular in the case of clients with relatively small media budgets, whose accounts nevertheless impose heavy demands of time and effort on the agency. There are, however, disadvantages in this system also, as will be seen.

Agency Costing. Advertising agencies are gradually becoming aware of the need for an efficient internal costing system which will enable them to distinguish more accurately between profitable and unprofitable business. Size of billing alone is not an infallible guide; frequently a large account can be less profitable, in real terms, than a small one. For this reason it is desirable that careful costing should be employed.

An agency's major expenditure item is salaries; consequently the most prominent feature of a costing system will be the allocation of labour time, with materials (that is, mostly studio materials) accounting for the rest. Other costs, such as rents (few agencies own the freehold of their premises), lighting, telephones, depreciation of office equipment, etc., will be allocated on the basis of size of account.

Thus, each department will keep as accurate a record as possible of the time each of its members spends working on each account, so that the agency's management can monitor the relationship of the proportion of total turnover provided by specific accounts to the proportion of total costs borne by those accounts. On the evidence of these figures, it may be necessary, from time to time, to resign accounts on grounds of unprofitability; or to ask for higher fees for services offered; similarly, it may be possible to consider accepting accounts which fall short of the minimum turnover limits sometimes imposed, rather arbitrarily, by agencies who use billing as the only yardstick.

Effective Account Management

It is obvious from what has been said that good campaign control (or account management) depends above all on the executive's ability to identify himself with his client's requirements and to maximise the achievement of his client's objectives. In so doing, he must anticipate every possible hazard and remove it; in a sense, the good executive must *expect* things to go wrong and put them right in advance, as an automatic part of his administrative function. On the other hand, account management is not merely a matter of administration; it is also a very creative operation. The best executive is the one who, faced as he is every day with a thousand new demands on his time, not all of them necessarily directly relevant to the central campaign, can still preserve his sanity sufficiently to stand back from the detail of the canvas and view the picture as a whole. In between writing work requisitions, checking budgets, reading proofs and meeting copy dates, he must be able to identify new opportunities for increasing his client's sales by taking tactical advantage of the chances offered and contributing himself to the creative input, not by writing words and drawing pictures but by imaginatively employing his promotional initiative. Such men are comparatively rare, but those that exist can significantly increase a client's success.

Campaign Evaluation

In this chapter we have examined the role of advertising in the context of our modern social environment; we have analysed the structure of the advertising agency; and we have illustrated the steps taken in the planning, implementation and supervision of an advertising campaign. In so doing, we have turned the wheel almost full circle, and we are now almost back at the point from which we started.

An advertising campaign, however, is not finished and forgotten when the final space has been filled, or the last television commercial transmitted. If the agency is to produce better and more effective advertising for the following year, it must be prepared to learn from what has happened. Advertising, as we have seen, is by no stretch of the imagination an exact science, and it relies still on inherently emotive values for its effectiveness and the measurement of its success or failure, despite many attempts to quantify and correlate its contributing effort. Thus it is largely on the experience of what has gone before that any campaign is judged to be good or bad; and it is for this reason that this chapter ends with what could be argued to be its beginning.

Advertising people, although they recognise that, outwardly, the only visible evidence of the success or failure of a campaign is the rise or fall of their client's sales graph, are nevertheless always anxious to judge it on less prohibitive and – admittedly – possibly more subjective criteria. It is true that advertising can contribute to sales sucess; it is equally possible that advertising can either have no effect on sales at all or cause them to fall. Yet it would be rash to equate advertising and sales too closely in causal terms; there are many other elements in the marketing 'mix' which can make an equally strong impact. Rosser Reeves, in his book *Reality in Advertising*, says: 'The product may be wrong. Price may be at fault. Distribution may be poor. The sales force may not be adequate. Budget may be too low. A better product may be sweeping the market. A competitor may be outwitting you with strong deals. There are many variables.' [1] Advertising, through the lack of a *direct* causal connection, cannot categorically be blamed for sales failure, nor, by the same token, praised for sales success.

For this reason, both during and after an advertising campaign, it is essential to obtain as much data as possible about the effectiveness of its communication. We saw how, in the planning stage, both concepts and specific copy were tested in advance; we shall see now that no

[1] Rosser Reeves, *Reality in Advertising* (New York: Knopf, 1961), p. 12.

testing programme is complete without validation of advertising in action.

Advertising evaluation falls broadly into two categories: firstly, tests designed to measure the degree to which a campaign has succeeded in communicating its message, and, secondly, research into the extent to which it has influenced consumer opinion and stimulated sales. We shall refer to the first category as advertisement post-testing and the second as advertising/sales correlation.

Advertisement post-testing. Some post-testing techniques are valid only if their results can be compared with similar data obtained before the campaign starts. Thus, if research is to be carried out to measure the level of recall of brand name or the degree of product awareness (often called 'penetration studies'), it is difficult to evaluate how effective a campaign has been unless information already exists on awareness levels before exposure to that campaign which will enable comparisons to be made.

Research such as this will be conducted, either on a national or regional (or, in the case of a test market, even on a town) basis, amongst a sample representative of the campaign's target audience. It will consist of questions formulated to discover the extent to which the different elements of the campaign have been communicated, in particular the association of brand name with product and selling proposition; in this way management will be able to establish, after comparing results with pre-campaign data, whether their product has been invested with the desired brand image in the consumer's mind. The survey will also measure consumer awareness of competitive products, and will thus provide indications of the comparative strength of product identities within the context of the total market.

The value of this kind of research should be obvious. While controlled tests of advertising material can be conducted before its exposure in campaigns proper, they can never fully establish that the material will achieve exactly the same effect under campaign conditions when other stimuli and constraints, perhaps unforeseen, will be operating. All that pre-testing can do is to supply evidence of probability that such-and-such a result will be achieved, which, in the event, is sometimes very far from the mark.

Thus, many years ago, when it was the fashion to promote the importance of bleach in washing powders, Lever Brothers decided to stress the fact that Oxydol, one of their brands, washed whiter *without* bleach, on the premise that it was the end, not the means, which was important to housewives. When a penetration study was carried out after the campaign had run, the company was surprised to find that Oxydol was recalled almost unanimously as 'the one with the bleach'. What had happened was that, despite pre-testing which had shown that housewives approved of bleach only because it made laundry white, the very mention of bleach in the campaign immediately created an association between it and the product.

Another example of unintentional campaign effect is the 'video vampire', a description coined by Rosser Reeves to refer to a visual element in advertising which, although designed to enhance and support the selling message, is so strong as to create recall of itself to the detriment of brand name or advertising claim. There was a year or two ago a cinema film promoting the bill-paying services of one of the major banks; its visual effect was very strong, showing a man becoming increasingly helpless with laughter as he opened bill after bill. The point was, of course, that he had no worries about paying his bills because he had opened a budget account at the bank – but which bank? Few people could remember.

Penetration studies, recall tests and the like are more than interesting exercises. They are (or should be) conducted as a guide to future action, like all research. Evidence from this type of research should be used to correct mistakes of creative implementation and to contribute to the formulation of future advertising strategy.

Another technique in common use as a means of testing advertising communication in real campaign conditions is that known as reading and noting studies. This differs from penetration research in that it is conducted during the campaign itself, and not necessarily after the build-up effect has had time to materialise; furthermore, it is essentially a technique for testing press advertising, whereas penetration and recall studies can be applied equally to press and television.

The reading and noting technique was developed by Gallup Poll many years ago to measure the effectiveness of press advertisements both overall and in specific detail – headline, sub-heads, main illustration, body copy, company or brand name, product illustration, etc. – and at the same time to analyse the relationship between the reading and noting scores of the advertisement and those of other advertisements and pages in the same newspaper or magazine.

The operation is carried out as follows. Gallup Poll draws up a programme of testing, indicating which issues of which publications will be subjected to reading and noting studies. Usually only mass circulation national publications are chosen, because it is through these that sample readers representative of national population characteristics will be found. Furthermore, restriction of the survey to such media enables Gallup to build up a store of comparative back data classified by product type and specific publications. Agencies are circulated with details of the testing programme, and as a result book client advertisements into specific issues to take advantage of the test data, which they buy from Gallup when the test has been completed.

Immediately after the publication of the issue in question (usually the next day), Gallup interviewers seek out people who claim to have read a copy and proceed to take them through each page, asking questions on what they remember having seen and, if they have read it, the detail of its content. The data emerging from this are classified into male and female readership, and relate to 'page traffic' (the percentage of men and women reading and noting *any* item on specific pages) as well as the scores for any piece of editorial matter or any advertisement and its component parts.

The Gallup presentation report to the agency analyses the scores for the agency's readership and compares them with scores for other advertisements of a comparable size in the same issue; in addition, it gives average ratings for advertisements for similar products in that publication (based on all issues ever previously tested) and the highest scores for similar products in that publication in the past. The agency is thus given criteria on which to judge its own efforts.

The results of reading and noting studies are less useful than those of recall tests, since the research is conducted with the object of examining advertisements from an almost entirely technical and mechanical standpoint. Whereas recall tests probe relatively deeply into the inferences and nuances of the communication process itself and actually indicate consumers' own perceptions and mental interpretations of advertising messages, reading and noting studies merely record whether or not an advertisement and the elements contained in it have been seen, irrespective of meaning or interpretation. Such studies therefore, are of use only as a guide to advertising layout, typography and artistic treatment, not as a validation of concepts or brand images.

Some newspapers and magazines offer advertisers a further opportunity for advertisement testing, known as 'split run' tests, although this is really a sophisticated form of pre-testing. Its purpose is simply to establish which of two advertisements works better. The publication allows the advertiser to place a different advertisement in different editions or alternate copies, each advertisement including a coupon which readers are asked to cut out and send in for a special offer or free booklet or more information. The coupons are keyed, and the advertisement from which the larger number of coupons is returned is presumed to be more effective, although it is not necessarily true that an advertisement evoking a greater coupon response is better at selling a product.

There are advertisers who depend entirely on coupons for advertising success. Examples are manufacturers selling direct to the consumer without an intermediate retailer (some domestic durable products – appliances, carpets, etc.), or financial services (insurance, unit trusts, building societies) or charities or correspondence courses. Such companies measure advertising success on sales per advertisement or, to be more exact, the ratio of sales to coupon returns per advertisement (coupon conversion factor). There is in such cases clearly no other yardstick than that of immediate results.

Advertising/Sales Correlation. It has already been pointed out that it is rash to assume too direct a causal connection between advertising and sales results because of the very many variables which can occur in the marketing mix. There have nevertheless been dozens of attempts to establish formal correlations of advertising expenditure and sales income, each attempt possibly more bizarre than the last. The great difficulty, of course, is that no two advertising budgets of similar size are spent in exactly the same way. What is more, the content of no two compaigns will be the same.

On the other hand, there is clearly *some* connection between advertising and sales, even though we may not be able to quantify it exactly, and it is the purpose of advertising evaluation to attempt to establish the broad relationship between the two.

The Retail Audit. There are two main sources of sales data, apart from manufacturers' sales records. One is the retail sales audit, which measures the flow of goods across the counter or (in the case of self-service outlets) off the shelves. It examines, through a panel of sample stores representative of the national total, retailers' purchases and stocks on a two-monthly audit basis for almost every grocery, confectionery, pharmaceutical, tobacco and liquor product, and processes the information obtained from invoice checks and stock counts to provide a full picture of retail sales, distribution and weeks' supply. It classifies this information on a shop size (multiple, co-operative, independent) basis, as well as by shop type (counter service, shop service, symbol member, etc.) and geographical location (standard region, television area), and sells it as a syndicated service to individual subscribers at so much per product or size. The retail audit is synonymous with the A. C. Nielsen Company, which pioneered the idea in the United States and now operates throughout the world. With industrial, as distinct from consumer, products such a system is clearly not possible on a syndicated basis. Individual companies, therefore, have to provide their own information source.

The Consumer Panel. The retail audit, useful and informative though it is, gives only one side of the picture: it shows where and in what volume products have been bought, but it gives no indication of what kind of people have bought them. This is the function of the consumer panel, which obtains information from a national sample of housewives on a monthly basis and is conducted through a combination of questionnaires and larder checks. Information is again supplied by area, but in addition it is classified by age and social class of housewife, as well as by reading and viewing habits.

The best-known panel of this type is the Attwood panel. One of its important uses, besides providing data on brand shares and volume purchased, is as a guide to brand switching: for example, if changes in brand shares over a month have occurred as follows:

	Month 1 (%)	*Month 2* (%)
Brand A	36	33
Brand B	27	30
Brand C	15	15
Others	22	22

the immediate assumption could be that Brand B has gained 3 per cent brand share from Brand A. However, it is possible from consumer panel information to detect movements within these figures which show a rather different picture:

	Share gained from/lost to				*Month*	*Net*
	A	*B*	*C*	*Others*	*2 shares*	*gain/loss*
	(%)	(%)	(%)	(%)	(%)	(%)
Brand A	—	−5	+1	+1	33	−3
Brand B	+5	—	−3	+1	30	+3
Brand C	−1	+3	—	−2	15	—
Others	−1	−1	+2	—	22	—

Thus, Brand B has gained almost twice as much from A as might have been assumed, while Brand C has gained 3 per cent from B but at the same time lost 1 per cent to A and 2 per cent to Others. Brand A has recouped some of its loss by taking 1 per cent from both C and Others. 'Hidden' movements such as this are important to marketing management in its analysis of sales results.

Through the retail audit and the consumer panel a comprehensive pattern of sales performance can be identified, but it will not be possible to relate this to advertising effort except in the most general terms. For instance, area sales variations can to a degree indicate the advisability or otherwise of regional budget weightings; they can also be used to judge the comparative effectiveness of one medium against another. However, sales research is rarely a sufficient guide to advertising performance if employed in isolation from other forms of evaluation, and furthermore it cannot provide any dependable information on the effectiveness of advertising content; it is no more than a crude measurement of budget efficiency.

Sales research's main contribution to advertising strategy lies in the planning function. Thus, information on distribution, area sales, breakdowns by shop type and size and housewife buying habits is an essential part of the apparatus of marketing data which provides the clues for future advertising policy.

Usage Pull. There is one technique which has been deliberately omitted from the foregoing examination; deliberately, because in view of the remarks about the difficulties and dangers of drawing too many conclusions from the relationship between advertising and sales it is interesting that this technique was devised specifically to obviate these hazards.

It is called the theory of usage pull, and was initiated by one of America's major agencies, Ted Bates and Co. Inc. of New York, after the Second World War. It is described enthusiastically by Rosser Reeves, the Bates chairman, in his book *Reality in Advertising*, which is a curious admixture of advertising copy (for Ted Bates) and some shrewd, sound commonsense.

The basis of the theory is simple, straightforward and attractive:

Conceive of the whole population of the United States divided into two huge rooms.

In one room put all the people who do *not* know your current advertising. They do not remember what it said; they do not recall having seen it, read it, or heard it; their minds, as far as your advertising is concerned, are complete blanks. Now, walk into this room and interview these people. Find out how many are using your product.

Let us say that 5 out of every 100 people who do not know your advertising (or 5 per cent) are customers.

Since these five people do not know your advertising, it is obvious that they must have chosen your product in another way. Perhaps a friend told them about it, or you gave them a free sample, or their doctor recommended it. Perhaps they were led to it by an old campaign which they have now forgotten. Perhaps they learned about it, as children, from their mothers and fathers. But they did not become customers as a result of your current advertising, because they do not know your current advertising.

Now, walk into the other room. Here are the people who *do* remember your advertising. They can prove that they know it, because they can tell you, correctly, what it says.

Let us say that 25 out of every 100 people who do know your advertising (or 25 per cent) are customers.

From 5 per cent to 25 per cent. Now you have one of the most exciting statistics in modern advertising. For it tells you that if you ran no advertising at all, for a while you would sell to 5 per cent of the people, but that *out of every 100 people who remember your advertising, an extra 20 are being pulled over to the usage of your product.*

The pulled *v.* the unpulled![1]

This, in Reeves's own words, is what the theory is all about; in practical terms, Bates have been collecting interview data across the United States for over twenty years, and correlating the penetration of dozens of major advertising campaigns with purchasing habits. The truths revealed by this research, says Reeves, are 'startling', and show that many much admired campaigns are doing little for their products, while some others, unspectacular and unnoticed by advertising people, are getting excellent results.

On the face of it, usage pull seems to provide exactly what advertising has been seeking – a direct causal link between the campaign and the sale, but unfortunately it is not as perfect as it sounds, for it is subject to some of the same potential errors as any other method. It ignores, for example, the influence of point-of-sale display; it does not take into account retailers' regional price cuts; it assumes perfect distribution patterns for all products; it overlooks variations in climate, in geography, in social attitudes; and it fails to consider advertising weight. It is, in short, prone to distortion by many of the variable factors which Reeves was trying to avoid. But it is at least an improvement on previous attempts to find the answer.

Forward Planning

Thus, like the farmer who has harvested his grain and carted his straw and begins to plough once more for next year's crop, the advertising men must start planning another campaign as soon as one is over.

All the facts, all the figures, all the successes and failures, the triumphs and the mistakes must be analysed and sifted. Without evaluation no campaign can stimulate the next. There are great dangers here: clients have a habit of getting quickly bored with a campaign approach – understandably, since they have lived very close to it for so long – but there is an old and well-tried maxim to the effect that when the client is tired of his advertising it is just beginning to work. The people who create and pay for advertising sometimes forget that their audience

[1] Rosser Reeves, *Reality in Advertising* (New York: Knopf, 1961), pp. 13–14.

sees far less of it than they do themselves; advertising rarely works immediately – it has a gradual and cumulative effect and cannot be measured in terms of budgetary years or fiscal periods. Communication is a continuous process, and awareness, recognition and subsequent action can take a very long time to develop.

It is easy for advertisers to want to change to something new, to inject a different identity into their products and to spread their efforts over a broader base and a wider audience. It is also very easy to kill a product stone dead in the process. Consider the most successful advertising themes, and remember how long their life has been: Katie and Oxo, Drinka Pinta Milka Day, the Homepride flour graders, Don't be Vague, and (from an earlier age) Guinness, Bovril and Lux.

In 1964 Ind Coope moved their Double Diamond account to a new agency because they felt that 'A Double Diamond works wonders' was dated and meaningless. A new campaign was mounted, with a new image and a new theme; it was doomed to failure because the old claim was too firmly established in the consumer's mind. In four years two further new campaigns were tried, despite increasing resistance from the company's sales force and incontrovertible research data that the old claim was still much stronger. The company finally gave in: they reverted to the 'works wonders' approach and moved the account once more.

This is a salutary tale. Unless the evidence is overwhelming there are always much better reasons for keeping to a consistent theme, even if not startlingly successful, than for changing to something different, because it is always easier to build on (even minimal) awareness than no awareness at all.

Naturally, campaigns need to be developed and renewed, but this will involve modifications and variations only of presentation, not of the central concept; one of the purposes of advertising evaluation is to assess the 'wear out' factor of specific advertisements so that changes of style can be effected at the most opportune moment.

The same philosophy is true of media planning: a change of media pattern (from press to television or vice-versa) is a break in continuity, and good reasons need to exist for it. There is, however, frequently an argument for changes of space size or length of television spot to accommodate a new or different presentation of the creative concept; much research has been done (in surveys of the reading and noting type) to establish the relative cost/readership ratios of full pages, half-pages and other display advertisement sizes when used in different ways.

Thus, the three requirements for successful advertising stipulated by Sir William Crawford, one of the great figures of British advertising in the earlier years of the twentieth century, are just as true today as when he wrote them: domination, concentration, repetition. Too many, alas, of today's advertisers appear to have forgotten his advice.

Chapter 3

The Search for Protection

The Growing Consciousness of Power

In the previous two chapters we have seen how advertising has developed from modest and almost accidental beginnings to a highly complex and organised mechanism. It has passed through many phases and has been forced many times to adapt itself in order to satisfy the changing needs of the industry it serves; it has also at times stimulated modifications and revisions of attitudes within industry itself, and is thus now to some degree duplicating the functions of its client companies, largely in the areas of marketing analysis and planning.

We have also seen how advertising agency profitability has fallen dramatically in the past few years. Most British agencies would be only too ready to admit that life is not as rosy as it was five years ago; there has been a wave of redundancies, rationalisations and reorganisations, all designed to maintain maximum profits and minimise overheads. This has been prompted by a tightening of clients' purse strings and a crippling increase in taxation (although the latter has now been somewhat alleviated by the reduction and eventual abolition of Selective Employment Tax). The result has been fairly predictable: small and medium-sized agencies, which, like their larger cousins but to a far more damaging extent, have felt bound to maintain their many service departments in the interests of competitive strength, have either gone out of business entirely or been forced to sell out to or merge with others in order to benefit from economies of scale. This has not always been successful, since it is by no means axiomatic that two small units joined together will be as effective as one large one; and it has been the large units which have attracted the big accounts. In advertising, as in the rest of industry, power has been concentrating into fewer and fewer hands.

Advertising has always been a rather sensitive business; that is to say, advertising people have traditionally been sensitive to comment and criticism. Ever since that day in 1841 when Volney Palmer first opened his doors as an advertising agent and established an anomalous precedent (wherein the word 'agent', while ostensibly referring to the responsibility the agency bears towards its clients, in effect means nothing more nor less than blood money from the media owners themselves), advertising seems always to have been on its guard to fend off attacks on its purpose and its practice.

Agencies (and particularly British agencies) have therefore always rightly felt the need for some kind of supervising authority, both in their own interests and in the interests of the clients they represent and the consumers to whom they communicate. They have realised and acknowledged the power they wield and the influence they can exercise, and it is not surprising that the growth of this power has given rise to a corresponding need for its protection.

This realisation of power has been manifested in a number of ways. One is the existence of various clubs, institutes and associations, the best known of which are the Institute of Practitioners in Advertising and the Advertising Association. The IPA provides several useful services for the industry, not least of all the availability of a standard examination system for young executives (under the auspices of CAM – Communications Advertising and Marketing Education Foundation), a fair amount of data on newspaper and magazine readership, a well-stocked library, participation in the television audience measurement service produced by Audits of Great Britain, and the opportunity for member agencies to be represented on its many committees which speak for the industry in negotiations and consultations with the Government and others – all for a fee, of course. Membership of the IPA is limited to agencies, and only to those who satisfy the Institute's requirements of status.

Unfortunately, this is by no means as Utopian as it sounds. More and more large and successful agencies either do not join the IPA (although qualified to do so) or have resigned from it. This tends to make something of a nonsense of the whole situation; one of the cornerstones of IPA protection is the regulation forbidding member agencies to solicit business from each other, but there is nothing to prevent a non-member from poaching accounts from a member or vice-versa. It could therefore be argued that, far from being a protection, membership of the IPA is a positive hindrance to the acquisition of new business. (Incidentally, it must be admitted that the IPA's rules on 'soliciting' are beautifully quaint: you are allowed to send a letter to a competitive agency's client, but you are not permitted to address him by name. In fact, it seems you can get away with almost anything short of walking into the client's office and openly demanding his business.)

The Advertising Association, on the other hand, has a wider membership, consisting not of companies but individuals from both agencies and industry. Its function is different, providing opportunities for executives to meet and discuss matters of interest and importance. It holds an annual conference at Brighton in a mixture of uninterrupted gloom and somewhat unhealthy self-congratulation, from which it is impossible to avoid the feeling that many advertising campaigns are written to impress other advertising people rather than to sell clients' products. Advertising people *en masse* are not in general an attractive congregation.

Another manifestation of advertising's awareness of its own importance is the rash of 'philosophies' – personal attitudes and memoirs – published by successful figures in the industry. The two best known examples of the genre in recent years have been David Ogilvy's *Confessions of an Advertising Man* and Rosser Reeves's *Reality in Advertising*. Both attempt to do the same thing, but set about it in very different ways; they are both anxious to expound, as a result of many years' practical experience, their views on what constitutes good advertising; they both concentrate, naturally enough, on creative attitudes and the mechanics of communication; but neither really produces what can truly be regarded as an exclusive advertising philosophy that can be applied without exception in any advertising situation.

Ogilvy bases his approach on two main creative requirements: advertising should arouse interest and attention, and it should build up an image and a personality for the product. Reeves, on the other hand, upholds the USP (the Unique Selling Proposition) as the secret ingredient: an advertisement must present a unique product quality, either truly unique (in the sense that no competitive product possesses it) or by pre-emption (in the sense that no competitive product is claiming it possesses it); this unique quality must be a benefit (that is, people must want to buy the product because of it); and this unique benefit must be communicated as a meaningful proposition.

There are many advertisements and campaigns which would satisfy both Ogilvy and Reeves, which have failed. There are many which would satisfy neither, which have succeeded. Yet both of them have attracted a large following, and it is not difficult to understand why: it is because advertising is not an exact science that its practitioners have grasped, if not in desperation, certainly with unconcealed enthusiasm the trappings and trimmings of the questionable formulae with which it is now bedecked. Of course there have been significant technical improvements, but they are in a sense only peripheral to the central function of the act of persuasion, which is essentially a matter of effective creative communication.

Advertising, in short, has ploughed an excessively uncertain furrow, everlastingly trying to prove itself and justify the power it has achieved, and succeeding often in the face of all reason. The success has been the success of a principle, not of an organised industry.

The Increasing Public Suspicion

There is no doubt that advertising has stimulated more public opprobrium and antipathy than any other business. We saw in the last chapter how many arguments have been advanced against advertising on various economic, moral, aesthetic and social criteria; for the most part, if any of these arguments have validity, it is only because sometimes advertising in practice does not always live up to its principles. Furthermore, almost without exception critics of specific examples of advertising in practice are criticising not so much advertising as the manufacturer whose products it is presenting. It is criticism, therefore, of abuse, not of use.

Yet what is surprising, when we analyse the reasons for advertising's blemished reputation, is that it has been achieved not solely through the evidence of advertisements themselves. The image still persists of a degenerate society, peopled by unscrupulous, indolent and overpaid playboys, parasitically existing on the gullibility of others, eating long and expensive lunches while they take time off from presenting the unsuspecting public with devilish and tempting propositions. The advertising fraternity, in many people's eyes, has about the degree of respectability of the white slave trade or illegal gun-running.

This startling image has grown gradually, and no more reflects the truth than the Hornblower stories describe conditions in the navy of today. It is the product of popular literature such as *The Hucksters* or any one of a score of lurid paperbacks on sale at the bookstalls; like many other stereotyped descriptions, it has lingered on long after its accuracy has disappeared, and while, as we have seen, the advertising business of the twenties and thirties may well have provided some justification for the 'hunches and lunches' label, there has never been an agency in real life quite as sensational or as fanciful as some fiction would have us believe.

Thus, although the cap is many sizes too large, advertising is thought to be wearing it. The books and the films still persist in portraying the business as thoroughly disreputable, the public reads the books and sees the films, and advertising constantly finds itself the object of a great deal of uninformed, and sometimes almost hysterical, comment.

If the criticism stopped there, little damage would be done, save for wounded pride; but it goes further. Advertising, it is claimed, for the sake of a quick profit, is prepared to distort and mislead, to lie and to subvert. Legislation is called for (there is already a 10 per cent surcharge on all television advertising): advertising expenditure should be subject to tax, like entertainment expenses, say the critics; there should be stricter controls on advertising, they cry, such as a limit on appropriations, fewer opportunities, more rigid supervision of content and even, according to some extremists, total abolition of advertising of every type.

This last suggestion, of course, is clearly absurd, since nobody can accurately define where advertising and other forms of communication divide: so-called 'government advertising', for example, such as the campaign for the Decimal Currency Board or the Common Market, or an announcement of increases in pensions, postal rates or National Insurance contributions, or the Road Safety campaign, or Premium Bonds announcements – which of these are advertising and which not? As L. W. Rodger puts it: 'A restaurant menu is strictly informative but is designed to persuade people to eat certain dishes. An omnibus timetable is designed to persuade people to travel by bus.'[1] All advertising is communication, but not all communication is advertising; the problem is to discriminate between the two.

Also, there would be more point to the desire to create restrictions on

[1] L. W. Rodger, *Marketing in a Competitive Economy* (Hutchinson, 1965), p. 180.

advertising practice, if there were no restrictions already. British advertising is possibly subject to more controls than that of any other country. In addition to the authority of the IPA itself, there is, as we have seen, a very strict watch over the products and services allowed on television and the way in which they can be featured; in addition, the IBA lays down stringent rules about the times at which specific products can be advertised (alcoholic drinks, cigars etc. – there is no advertising for cigarettes). The NPA (Newspaper Publishers' Association) requires its members to vet all advertising submitted to them, and gives them the right to reject any which they regard as untrue, misleading or dangerous. In the case of pharmaceutical products, all advertising material, both for press and television, must be submitted before publication (and preferably before production) to the PAGB (Pharmaceutical Association of Great Britain), without whose approval of its accuracy and intent it cannot be published.

There is also the recently enacted Trade Descriptions Act, which empowers all local Weights and Measures inspectors (or, indeed, any members of the public) to prosecute any company which, in their opinion, is guilty of misleading advertising. An action may be brought by an inspector in any area, and there is no guarantee, if a manufacturer is cleared by a court in, say, Bristol, that he will not be prosecuted on exactly the same grounds in Bridlington. This Act applies just as much to labelling, packaging and point-of-sale material as it does to media advertising.

Not long ago, all those sections of industry and commerce with interests in advertising produced the British Code of Advertising Practice, and it has been agreed that any advertisement offending against the standards thus established will not be accepted by the media. The Code is supervised by the Advertising Standards Authority, composed of people inside and outside advertising, with an independent chairman, and applied by the Code of Advertising Practice Committee.

If official controls should by any chance fail to detect falsehood, misrepresentation or abuse, there are independent bodies which are very ready to take up the standard, in the form of consumer protection organisations such as the Consumers' Association; and every citizen who suffers as a result of misleading advertising can call upon his rights in Common Law. The net is thus a very fine one, and little, if anything, can slip through it.

As John Hobson said in a lecture given to the Royal Society of Arts:

It is a system which is as watertight as it can be. It may not prevent some fly-by-night advertiser from offering spurious wares in some obscure local medium but it will go a long way to preventing serious abuses. . . . The balance of strength between the drive of the seller for more sales, and the natural caution and resistance of the buyer (which is in fact the current balance, and which has grown up in a free society over many centuries), is still the best system, and cannot be replaced by externally imposed limitations on either the buyer or the seller. In this balance of strength, salesmanship and advertising, which is mass salesmanship, play their part on behalf of the seller; and caution, inertia and habit as well as judgement, play their part for the buyer. No one should ever underrate the capacity of the British public to divine and assess the true values of what it is offered. It is erroneous as well as patronising to think it can be easily fooled. The public is very adult and can be treated as such. This is not to say that within this pattern there is not a case for every reasonable limitation on unfair selling and every possible protection for incautious or ignorant buying; and these precautions are being more and more devised by all concerned in the business. But we know this pattern works; all the alternatives are untried.

The Desire for 'Professionalism'

While few advertising people would admit to the opinion that their status is similar to that, say, of an architect, this is certainly the impression they convey. It is impossible to avoid the suspicion that advertising is almost desperately trying to justify itself and its relationship with the industries it exists to serve, a feeling caused partly perhaps by the IPA's (no doubt inadvertent) projection of the image of a professional body – on the same level as the Law Society or the British Medical Association.

It is, of course, absurd that a business which draws its remuneration not from the clients whom it represents but the suppliers from whom it buys space and time should ever think of itself as a profession. Yet almost every day men both inside and outside the industry use the term, either because they believe it to be accurate or because they are unthinkingly following the example of others; in either event it is a misnomer.

At the beginning of my career, I was asked by a wise old advertising manager why it was that I wanted to go into advertising, and while I was trying to think of a reply which would be at once truthful and unpretentious he volunteered a reason himself: 'Because it is more gentlemanly than industry.'

Although this is perhaps not the answer I was going to give, there is a lot of truth in it. Advertising has many connotations that industry lacks: it overlaps into many areas which are themselves professions – art and design, journalism and psychology, for example – and frequently imports employees from them. It does not deal in manufactured goods, it has no plant or machinery, its products are ideas and its only material assets are the people who produce the ideas. I have frequently taken visitors – prospective clients, students or just people who are curious to see what goes on – round the various departments of an advertising agency, and were it not for the studio nothing would distinguish the occupants from those of any other organisation (a civil service department or the head office of a bank); in a manufacturing organisation visitors can be shown the product taking shape – cans being filled, components being assembled or sweets being wrapped.

It is this one-stage removal from the material evidence of industry which gives advertising its peculiar identity and tempts so many people, both inside and outside its boundaries, into describing it as a profession. The IPA, as has been suggested, does little to contradict the fallacy; in fact, by encouraging an increasingly introspective and inbred attitude amongst its members, it has aped the procedures and principles of truly professional bodies, while at the same time it has failed to present advertising for what it is and for what it should be regarded as being – a service industry.

Lest it should be thought that this is meant to imply that the IPA is deliberately deluding itself, it must be stressed that the IPA has the interests of the industry very much at heart; it is, however, undeniable that the net effect of its attitude is to create the wrong image. It is often said that the product which advertising sells worst is itself; here is the prime example.

It may be argued that it matters little what advertising is called, providing it performs its function effectively, that the argument is a semantic one only; this is not so, because, like the legal profession, advertising could (and in some respects already does) begin to regard existing structures and practices as permanent and unchangeable. This is a dangerous attitude which through its complacency, however agreeable and satisfactory the present climate may be (and the past few years have shown the barometer to be falling fast), could lead to trouble.

Advertising, then, is very much a business, a part of the total industrial complex, and its practitioners, whatever else they may happen to be, should be primarily businessmen. An agency will be called upon to work for clients in many different fields, from washing machines to weed-killers, from motor cars to marmalade, from liquorice to life insurance, and it will discover and be given much privileged information about these clients; it will be required to keep such information to itself, like a doctor or solicitor, and not to leak it out to competitive companies. The reason has nothing to do with professional conduct: it is just good sound business sense.

Recruitment and Training

It is not uncommon to hear the question 'What makes a good doctor?' or 'What makes a good teacher?' or 'What makes a good engineer?' People have even been known to ask 'What makes a good advertising man?'

Until comparatively recently, as we have seen, advertising (for those who were in it) was rarely a deliberate career; it was something into which people drifted from something else. Perhaps as recently as ten years ago the average advertising agency consisted of a fairly equal mixture of untrained (but experienced) and trained (but relatively inexperienced) executives. Nowadays (since few people seem to stay in advertising until retirement age) the emphasis is very much on the trained executive who has made a deliberate decision to make advertising his career. It is an industry of young men: sucess will have been achieved before the age of thirty.

Selection and recruitment for creative staff, such as copywriters and artists, is handled by creative directors and group heads. Artists will come either from design work outside advertising (illustrators, design studio staff, etc.) or from one of the schools of art or design. In the latter case they will start by working on the more routine tasks of pasting down artwork, cutting masks, simple lettering, or adapting existing advertisements to different sizes, before embarking on original creative work of their own.

Copywriters will be recruited from two sources: they will either be taken on as trainees (graduate or otherwise) to be schooled in agency procedures preparatory to specialisation in writing; or they will be employed on the evidence of writing ability in their school or university days. Some are still recruited from journalism.

Advertising creative staff need to be able to do more than just draw or write. Indeed, it is sometimes argued that these abilities are of secondary importance. What *is* important is that they should possess creative minds, that they should be able to express ideas in visual form, verbal or otherwise, and that they should have the facility both to create concepts and translate them into active and persuasive communication.

Modern agencies – certainly the large ones – today devote much time, effort and expense to locating and training staff, sometimes only to see these same people leave the company after a couple of years to join another organisation. Although there is a higher turnover of staff in advertising than in most other industries (the average length of service is under two years and staff turnover can be as high as 40 per cent a year) and although there always seems to be a much greater supply of staff than the demand, good people are difficult to find. This is partly because the industry has been making do with fewer people so as to minimise overheads, and partly because it has significantly raised its standards over those of a few years ago.

The other specialist departments such as media and research naturally recruit staff as and when the need arises in specific functional areas – statisticians in particular – and, when new trainees are required, either they are selected from those of the agency's annual intake who wish to make media or research their special study or promotions are made from lower positions in other departments of people who have shown particular signs of promise (production assistants, traffic clerks and messenger boys).

By far the most difficult area of recruitment and training, however, is that for account executives and marketing men. In most large agencies these are synonymous, since, as we have indicated, specialist marketing departments these days are analyst departments, staffed by statisticians, econometricians and researchers. The modern account executive is (or should be) a marketing man in his own right, fully conversant with problems of market segmentation, buyer behaviour, pricing policies, channels of distribution, product planning, sales organisation and (naturally) all aspects of advertising and sales promotion.

The reasons for the difficulty in finding suitable account group staff is twofold: firstly, their knowledge and responsibility cover a very broad field; secondly, as we saw in the previous chapter, they have to work in that delicate area between client and agency where loyalties are not always simply defined and where tact and diplomacy are always essential. Their selection is thus a problem, because, although it may be possible to discover someone with the ability to assimilate the expertise necessary to the function, he may lack the qualities required to exercise that knowledge.

Thus, the average account executive tends to be first and foremost an administrator, since unless he is able to control and co-ordinate the routine functions of everyday activity the agency's efficiency will deteriorate and the client will quickly lose confidence through unsatisfactory service. It is a pity that the security of an account executive's position depends so much on this administrative ability, because a really imaginative and creative thinker at such a central point can contribute significantly to strategic and tactical policy and his client's profitability. Furthermore, it frequently happens that, even when an exective does possess the ability to identify and take advantage of promotional opportunities, he is prevented from doing so by the demands of his more mundane responsibilities.

The account executive needs to be a marketing man; but he needs his marketing skills in order to see his advertising problems in the proper perspective, as a backcloth against which his advertising activity can be created, implemented and evaluated. The marketing man *per se* – i.e. the client – needs them for their own sake; his function *is* marketing, and advertising is only part of it.

Ideally, therefore, the best account executives will come from industry, men who have had experience of the total marketing process, who can construct advertising objectives as part of the entire marketing 'mix' and who can look further than the immediate creative idea or media plan. It is, however, ironic that where the agency most needs such experience it is seldom found – for the reason we remarked earlier, that a good marketing man will find a fuller and more rewarding opportunity to exercise his talents elsewhere. This, as we shall see in a later chapter, may be more than just a cross which advertising has to bear; it may well stem from a basic irrelevance in modern agency operation and structure, for there is no doubt that there is a great deal of unnecessary duplication of effort.

How, then, do agencies recruit their executive staff, and how can they ensure that executives possess the skills necessary for the proper execution of their responsibilities?

Most large agencies take in each year one or more university graduates – usually arts graduates – to be trained in advertising techniques and systems. Most (indeed virtually all) of these finish up as assistant account executives after a period of about six months. They have no previous marketing experience; their awareness of the problems facing salesmen, retailers, production men or cost accountants is limited to the occasional day out with a client's representative or a visit to the factory; this background ensures a lively intelligence and an ability to assimilate the requirements of the functions they are shown within the agency, but the one essential ingredient is missing – practical experience of hard marketing activity in the place where it has reality and relevance, the manufacturing industries. Their marketing knowledge and expertise, in other words, has never been put to the practical test; it is in a way academically brittle.

Nothing can really be a substitute for knowledge gained through experience, especially in marketing, which is the fulcrum on which successful businesses rest; but in the absence of this experience, if advertising agencies are going to continue to operate in the way they do now, there is a strong case to be made out for sponsorship of trainee executives on post-graduate business (and especially marketing) courses, where they can at least be given the chance to obtain an infinitely broader business discipline than is possible within the narrower confines of the agency itself. The agency and its clients would both benefit, and the cost of training would quickly be amortised by the executive's improved performance (there would be a cost saving in any case through not having to devote time and personnel to trainee supervision). I suspect, however, that such a policy finds little favour with the general run of agency management; staff turnover is high, and many young executives change to a new agency after a very short stay with their first employer. There is a fear that others will reap the benefit of the investment. But then this works both ways.

The Danger of Protection

This constant growth from within, this grass roots policy in advertising may certainly protect the industry from invasion by other forces, but its effect in the long term is an increasing isolation from reality and a compounding of the almost mystical attitudes which have developed so rapidly of late. By preserving its incestuous structure in the face of the changing needs of business and by for ever building taller barriers to defend itself against growing suspicion, advertising is in danger of appearing to protest too much.

PART II

Chapter 4

Agency Anomalies

The Commission System

There have been many references in the earlier chapters of this book to the way in which advertising agencies earn their money. It will be remembered that, like many other facets of the business, the principle of agency 'commission' dates back to the formation of the first 'agency' in 1841 and has continued to be the basis of revenue ever since, applying equally to media and production expenditure alike.

If we examine the two words 'agent' and 'commission', we find that they have taken on different meanings in the context of advertising from those that apply elsewhere. An estate 'agent' takes a 'commission' on the sale of a house, but his client is the person for whom he is the agent and from whom he takes his commission; the buyer of the property has no contractual agreement with the agent, nor does he pay the agent for finding him the house. The same is true of an insurance 'agent': his 'agency' is for the insurance company on whose behalf he sells a policy.

Now while it may be argued that in 1841 Volney Palmer was an 'agent' (in the same sense as an estate agent or an insurance agent) for the newspapers for whom he solicited advertising space, there is no doubt that, as the arrangement stands today, the advertising agency's first responsibility is to its clients. Indeed, manufacturers commonly speak of '*our* agency' or '*our* advertising agents', and talk of 'paying commission' even though that commission is a rebate from media owner to the agency; to interpret current parlance in any other way would be pedantic and unrealistic, especially since most agency media departments spend a large proportion of their time fending off approaches from press and television representatives who are trying to sell their space and air-time.

This argument about words is not merely semantic: it is precisely because of this definition of the relationship between clients, agencies and media owners that the bizarre financial arrangement exists. In a sense it is a restrictive practice, since a small advertiser seeking what he believes to be the best service is frequently turned away by large agencies on the grounds that his budget is too small to provide an economic return; many agencies are in the habit of setting minimum budget levels below which no new account will be accepted. The agencies are thus guilty of the charge which they level against many of their clients: they are 'product-orientated', not 'customer-orientated'. In other words, they have decided what to sell before assessing what the market wants, because they are too committed to the constraints of tradition and too inflexible to satisfy an obvious demand. It is perhaps appropriate to ask whether an estate agent would set such minimal levels or whether an insurance agent would only sell policies above a certain value.

What is even worse is that many agencies are already handling business at a loss, some of them without even being aware of the fact. Agencies are not on the whole cost-conscious organisations: that is, few of them are able to say with any accuracy or certainty how much it costs them to handle specific accounts. Minimum budget requirements are in the main laid down arbitrarily (certainly not as the result of any system of costing such as was discussed in Chapter 2), and in those cases where costing exercises have been carried out there have been some ironic consequences: for example, an agency recently conducting such an analysis, using a client's computer for the purpose, discovered that the account of the client whose computer they were using was running at a loss of £6,000 a year.

I remember the chairman (and owner) of an advertising agency, for whom I once worked, saying quite genuinely that he did not really care how profitable or unprofitable individual accounts could be proved to be as long as they built up his turnover: let us first cover our overheads, he said, and everything thereafter will be profit. Well, of course this is true in one sense – that if revenue falls below costs the result is a loss. But there is little sense in cultivating business which costs more to handle than it produces in revenue, and there were several of his accounts which fell into this category. The clients, whose accounts these were, could not of course be expected to realise the situation: they were fortunate in having an agency which was as ignorant as themselves.

One of my own accounts had a gross annual billing of £2,000 and occupied as much of my time as another spending £50,000.

By the same token, when (as often happens) an agency 'rationalises' its business and resigns small accounts in order to concentrate on 'more profitable' clients, it may be a case of throwing away the baby with the bathwater; for it is not impossible that some of the accounts which remain are less profitable than some of those cast aside.

In another agency (not the one to which reference has just been made) it was decided that an account which billed only £5,000 should be resigned. The reason given was that it produced little or no profit and the client was unwilling to accept a fee arrangement. The truth of the matter was, however, that the £5,000 was spent in one publication and with one advertisement repeated several times: the creative team working on the account spent approximately an hour a year devising the content of the advertisement, the media group repeated its plan from year to year and devoted one telephone call and five minutes of a copy typist's time to booking the schedule, and artwork and production costs, though small, yielded a full 15 per cent profit. The executive group hardly noticed the account's existence and the agency made – *pro rata* – more money on that small account than on any other business it handled.

The reason for this apparent paradox is that although on paper each account shows a consistent 15 per cent gross revenue, the wide differences in time consumption from one account to another produce considerable variations in net profit; and since agency profitability (as we have seen) averages at under 2 per cent the variation needs to be only slight to overstep the profit/loss border. In this way an account representing, say, 5 per cent of an agency's turnover and only accounting for 1 per cent of its time can be more profitable than an account representing 15 per cent of turnover and 20 per cent of time.

Yet a properly structured costing system will allow an agency only to make the best of a bad job, so long as the commission system remains the basis of revenue. It will show which accounts are earning profits and which not, but it cannot evaluate the likely profit contribution of an account *before* the agency accepts it, nor can it be used for the purpose of establishing minimum acceptable budget levels except in a very general way. It is thus useful only in specifying which accounts to dispense with; it cannot identify which to accept.

The only way out of the dilemma, of course, is to change the basis of revenue by adopting an alternative system which will allow agencies to examine carefully in advance the likely volume of work on a given account and to assess the proportion of the agency's total working time that this volume will represent. On the strength of this, the agency will be able to establish a figure based on real costs and added profit. This fee will be the right price for the job, and not, like a commission, divorced from the realities of the situation.

Some agencies are already adopting fee arrangements for small accounts, but few have yet accepted the principle as the normal basis of business. Old habits die very hard, and the IPA is still firmly wedded to the commission system as the basic method of agency remuneration; therefore, in most of those agencies where fees are operated, the bulk of accounts is worked on commission. This is an uneasy compromise which will take time to resolve.

One of the reasons why commissions are in most cases retained is that agencies suspect that if a fee were negotiated it would be at a lower level than the income from commission. If this is so, it is yet further proof of the irrelevance of the commission system, since it can clearly produce excessive, as well as inadequate, income levels. It is another indication that commissions bear no relation to the work involved.

Another argument against the adoption of fees is not only that they have to be based on a very detailed and highly specific definition of the work they represent, but also that this definition needs frequent re-examination and reassessment to ensure that work levels are not falling short of or exceeding those originally stipulated. Far from militating against the fee system, this argument presents a strong case in its favour, for it not only ensures that clients are always getting the service for which they pay but also that the agency always gets a fair price for its work.

In this context, it is perhaps worth pointing out that even under the commission system it is not uncommon for agencies and clients to argue about charges. Indeed, some clients are so suspicious of the legitimacy of their agency's charges that they insist on receiving, with their monthly accounts, copies of the invoices their agencies have received from suppliers. By these means they are able to verify that they are not being charged over the odds for work done, and that their agents are not making more than the stipulated 15 per cent on their expenditure.

Surely, if the need for such scrutiny exists, it suggests that the present commission arrangement is far from satisfactory and that some alternative must be found which will assure a client that his account is being handled efficiently and honestly. Until such a situation is achieved there will inevitably be friction and dissatisfaction, which can be resolved only by a fair and equitable fee agreement.

It goes without saying that, under a fee agreement, all commissions received by the agency are automatically rebated to the client. This has the additional benefit of simplifying accounting procedures, since suppliers' invoices to the agency correspond exactly with those from the agency to the client. The fee is invoiced on a monthly basis, and thus provides the agency with a consistent level of income unaffected by the seasonal variations of media expenditure.

The current situation, therefore, is one of uncertainty, or, at best, transition. The agencies have for too long accepted unquestioningly the traditional systems and attitudes on which the industry is based, and it will be some time before they have reconciled themselves fully to the changed environment. The years since the Second World War have been, for business, perhaps more significant than any period other than the industrial revolution, for quite apart from the bewildering advances in technology, which have revolutionised both the processes and the products of manufacturing industries and increased the efficiency and profitability of services, there has been a broader and deeper understanding of the principles upon which businesses are run. No company these days can survive unless it thinks and plans five years ahead; industry cannot any more succeed on the here-today-gone-tomorrow outlook which bedevilled it for so long. As in so many other facets of life, the evolutionary process has been accelerated; man is now master of his own future: and survival depends not so much on being the fittest, as if through some uncontrollable natural plan, but on the determination, knowledge and foresight to become so.

Advertising is an intrinsic part of both the social and industrial scene. As such, it must inevitably change as society and industry change, and the old ideas must disappear. No other part of industry could hope to survive in the seventies on the financial attitudes of present-day advertising. The commission system produces ignorance, uncertainty, inefficiency and instability; the fee system offers precision and profitability.

The Marketing v. *Creative Dilemma*

In the first chapter it was pointed out that agency marketing departments, having flourished and proliferated during the second decade after the war, are now for the most part employed only as analyst groups; furthermore, in the second chapter, in the section on training and recruitment, it was shown that account group personnel have themselves largely taken over the marketing planning role within the agency, using their marketing knowledge to further the accurate deployment of their client's advertising effort – in agencies, that is, which can lay any claim to objective attitudes.

There can be no doubt that this represents a duplication of effort. Sometimes there can be a benefit in more than one person offering comments on specific data with a view to the implementation of a tactical course of action, such as, for example, the sales manager, the research manager, and a creative director; each will look at the situation from his own specialist viewpoint and they may possibly stimulate each other to reach a better conclusion than they might have reached individually. The important word is 'specialist': the three men are specialists in their respective functional areas of selling, research and creative work. The account director, on the other hand, is not a specialist, unless marketing in this context is a specialism.

The real question is to what extent it is necessary to have two separate centres of strategic decision making. It is questionable, in the case of companies where the standard of marketing management is high, whether anyone from the agency is capable of offering better (or even equally good) advice on marketing policy. An able and efficient product manager, in a team which can organise and control the company's marketing effort, needs no help from an agency account group other than the work of co-ordination which that account group has to perform in looking after its clients' interests.

It may be argued that this is in direct contradiction to what was said in Chapter 2 about the functions of account management within an agency, and to some extent it is. Account groups still need to make a positive and constructive contribution to client marketing policy, but this is invariably in instances where the client himself, either because he has not yet reached the proper level of marketing development or because he cannot yet afford to employ men of high marketing skills, is unable adequately to do the job himself. These are much fewer in number than most agency people believe.

In contrast, there are some companies which almost arrogantly spurn the offer of marketing help from their agency. It would be invidious to quote names, but an example will lose nothing through anonymity. I recently listened to a paper given to an audience of teachers of marketing from British business schools by an executive from one of the largest American-owned packaged goods companies whose products are household names in every home in this country. He made no secret of the fact that decisions on virtually all aspects of marketing planning which relate to the advertising function are made without the help of his company's agencies; the agencies have to do as they are told. True, they provide a creative service, but in all other respects they are closely monitored, even guided, by the client. This is particularly true of media planning: the agency accepts without question the client's detailed instructions on the regional deployment of the budget or the ratio of peak/off-peak television spots.

Many companies – Unilever, Beechams, Lyons – have their own media departments which supervise their agencies' media buying. Some even negotiate discounts direct with the media themselves. The more sophisticated companies feel very confident that they can turn their hand to any advertising function except the creative one.

Yet in spite of this openly admitted duplication of effort, why does it still exist? Instead of doing something to rationalise the situation, advertisers on the whole seem to make excuses for it. Presumably they feel that it is a problem the agencies need to sort out for themselves – after all, it is the agencies who choose to bear the financial burden of uneconomic organisation, not their clients. But as more clients improve their marketing skills the problem will be aggravated to a quite intolerable degree, and clients must sooner or later realise that they too have a financial burden, that of paying for service which they neither use nor need.

Perhaps the area in which all this is most apparent is in the development of new products, never a strong point with advertising agencies because they are called in at a stage when most of the groundwork has been accomplished. Consequently most agency executives are largely ignorant both of the new product development process and the relationships it involves with other functional areas such as production and finance. There are, of course, one or two of the larger agencies who have new product departments, but these merely exacerbate the problem of duplication.

New product development places agencies right on the horns of the dilemma. On the one hand, they feel that they should claim some relevance in this area since otherwise their marketing repertoire may seem to be incomplete; and on the other hand, what most of their clients want above all else is a good creative idea, not marketing expertise. Thus even in those cases where an agency's new product development group may be used by clients, it is creative concepts, not product concepts, which are being sought. Maybe, if agencies were to present a more positive identity in this vital area by shedding their uncertainty and opting for either purely creative work on new products or a comprehensive and integrated new product development service, their role would be more acceptable.

The real root of the problem is that the agencies, in attempting to present the impression of all-round ability, have succeeded only in drawing attention to their inadequacies and have failed to recognise their strengths. They have also incidentally failed to appreciate that, while they have been trying to justify themselves in areas in which their clients are much better equipped, their clients have been more alert to the realities of life: few clients will deny that they need help in the creation of their advertising message; they argue that, although they are perfectly competent to handle every other aspect of their marketing planning, creative matters are best left to the experts.

Thus we can make out a strong case for insisting that advertising agencies should concentrate on what they can do best – that is, the creative work which the rest of industry avoids because it requires an expertise of a very special kind. While advertisements may be only the tip of the iceberg of planning, they are nevertheless the only part of it that is judged by the outside world because it is the only part that is visible. Without good creative interpretation of an agreed marketing concept, the concept itself might just as well never have been agreed; and it is only advertising which has the ability and the experience to supply this creativity.

It may be asked: why, if clients feel able to cope with all the other facets of the advertising function, do they feel unable to take this final step? The answer is that it is a step into (for them) uncharted territory.

They can evaluate their new product development programmes, they can cost and analyse their sales, they can assess their distribution channels, they can identify their research needs, and they can even design and buy their media schedules – because these activities depend on principles which are intrinsically no different from the principles on which every other aspect of their business is based. They are concrete, quantifiable processes which, while they require both judgement and imagination if they are to be carried out successfully, are nevertheless capable of accurate measurement; they are mechanical, frequently boring and predictable areas of management decision.

The creative process, on the other hand, is different. By definition, it involves ideas, invention, subjectivity. It is personal, although it must always try to mirror other personalities. It is often inspirational, sometimes even irrational. It can be gay or sad, cultured or vulgar, flippant or serious. It requires a mind which thinks in premises, not conclusions. It is more emotional than cerebral. It is concerned less with form than meaning, less with exactitude than impression, less with description of detail than with communication of thought.

Such an activity would be an uneasy bedfellow for the management of most firms. The attitudes and behaviour which are found in client companies would not comfortably accept the alien principles of creative people. The two are incompatible within the same organisation; it is inconceivable for there to exist two sets of rules.

It is therefore not only better but more effective for the two to be separate, each in its own element. This way, the client can accept more readily the difference of attitude. Research and media activities have a logical place in his company, because they are consistent with all else that he does; creative activity does not, because it is a separate world, a world he prefers to keep apart, to consult only when necessary, not a continuing and dynamic pulse in his system of things.

Thus we can see that the dilemma is a very real one, but not recognised as such by the agencies. The steps they are taking, the general direction of their thinking, the currents of indecision, all point to movement to a misguided purpose. The proper answer lies in the opposite quarter; they should accept the facts as they are, not as they would like them to be; they should concentrate on the preservation of their acknowledged creative expertise, and save themselves the trouble and frustrations of fighting a war that is already lost on other fronts.

The New Business Business

The third major anomaly in advertising is the business of getting new business. This has already been referred to briefly in the previous chapter, but it must be examined in some depth.

All advertising agencies need to have some sort of official recognition before they can qualify for the commission allowed by the media owners on the placement of press, television, radio and outdoor bookings. The recognition generally held to be the most respectable is membership of the IPA, which is dependent on at least one director of the agency being a MIPA himself (of course, it is by no means exceptional for an agency not to belong to the IPA even if it is qualified to do so, as we have already seen). The IPA offers other so-called benefits in addition to eligibility for commission.

Besides recognition by the IPA, there are other degrees of eligibility, each in its own way offering some commission privileges. The NPA (Newspaper Publishers' Association) and the NS (Newspaper Society) both recognise agencies for discounts on newspaper bookings; the PPA (Periodical Proprietors' Association) allows commission to its members on space booked in magazines; and the ITCA (Independent Television Companies' Association) makes a similar dispensation to its members for air-time bookings. The criteria upon which agencies are judged to be eligible for membership of these bodies differ in detail, but depend more than anything on the volume of expenditure handled by individual agencies, the ability of those agencies to pay the bill, and the importance of their clients.

Whatever the rights or wrongs of these strictures, their existence is a fact which cannot be ignored; but what we are more concerned about here is the pressure exerted by one of them in particular – the IPA – on the business ethics of its members, specifically in the area of seeking new clients.

Clearly, every advertising agency must be on a constant lookout for new sources of revenue. Existing clients may remove their accounts, or budgets may be drastically reduced; either means a loss of profit, and since the agency's cash flow situation has to be controlled several months in advance this can result in a serious (in some cases fatal) financial situation. Furthermore, it has been estimated that in order to maintain profits at a constant level, an agency needs to increase its turnover at a rate of about 17 per cent per annum, to take account of rising prices and depreciation; translated into live terms, this means an extra £170,000 billing on each £1 million turnover, a fairly substantial target.

It is not therefore surprising that agencies seek every means they can find of attracting new clients. Some agencies have fewer problems than others, of course; there is certainly some truth in the old adage that 'success breeds success' in the advertising business. Once an agency's reputation has been established it is almost as difficult to lose as it was to gain in the first place: Hobson Bates is an excellent case in point – since its initial breakthrough with accounts like Cadbury, Nabisco, Lyons and Colgate it has grown almost without wanting to, adding household names to its account portfolio by the dozen. Agencies such as this frequently grow exponentially, and almost automatically find themselves on prospective clients' short lists when accounts are on the move. This is obviously a very satisfactory position to be in; the fact that clients largely come of their own accord means that the agency's management can concentrate on doing their best for the clients already on their books without the distractions of new business getting.

This happy state of affairs, however, is found in very few agencies. Perhaps only half a dozen or so have the enviable experience of being *invited* to make new business presentations without having to spend a great deal of time, effort and money on the preliminary softening-up process. Most agencies find that they must work very hard in a number of ways to acquire new accounts, and even then finish up with more failures than successes.

David Ogilvy, in his book,[1] has some revealing things to say about new business acquisition. His account is perhaps somewhat larger than life, in that he is describing an American, not a British, situation and he is thus removed from the inhibitions which could apply to an advertising agency chairman whose company is subject to the regulations imposed by the IPA. It is difficult to believe that circumstances were quite as orderly and convenient as he portrays them: it is all very well to concentrate on certain blue chip accounts and to ignore the fortuitous pickings of business life, notching the predestined successes on the stock of the gun as they fall, one by one, in their appointed order. Things never quite work out as neatly as this; but at least he made a point: no agency

[1] *Confessions of an Advertising Man* (Longman, 1964).

can really succeed in its new business progression without some sort of target – just as no advertising campaign can succeed without first of all having been directed at a correctly defined audience with a precise purchase proposition.

Ogilvy's success (and it has been a considerable success, despite the justification of hindsight and the literary rationalisation) has been due to his successful handling of the business he has obtained; the first lesson in advertising agency management is that an account in the hand is worth any number in prospect. More accounts than most agencies care to remember have been lost as a result of over-concentration on the new business problem and a corresponding neglect of the business on the books – understandable but unforgivable. Ogilvy realised that for his agency to prosper it must serve its existing clients as well as it could, for only in this way could he hope to prove to others that his company was capable of appreciating, defining and solving problems. Perhaps some of his methods are flashy, perhaps some of his stories are tall, perhaps (even) some of his friends and clients are less convinced of his infallibility than he is himself; but nobody can deny that he has achieved much. By his efforts he has carved out for himself a permanent niche in the history of American advertising and, as a Briton, has beaten the Americans – those traditional trend-setters in the business – fairly and squarely at their own game. For this he deserves not a little credit, even though he may in retrospect have made his performance appear rather easier than he is prepared to confess.

There are as many ways of getting new business as there are accounts, but they all tend to be variations on four main methods. An agency may advertise its talents in the national or trade press; it may use direct mail to prospective clients; it may involve itself in public relations activities – press releases, receptions, advertising awards, etc.; or its management may cultivate personal relationships with the executives of client companies. It is probably true to say that it is the last which brings in more new business than the other three; indeed, many agencies often employ new executives less for their ability than for their contacts, to wit, the many accounts that have changed agencies along with their account director.

Little needs to be said about the first two methods of getting business. They are all perfectly legal according to the regulations of the IPA, providing that no personal solicitation is involved. If I send promotional material through the post, it must clearly be a circular rather than a personal letter, and it must deal with the general proposition of my agency's ability rather than its specific application to the recipient's business. Why this should be, only the IPA knows; it clearly stems from the professionalism complex which was discussed in the previous chapter, but it is unexpected in a business which devotes its entire efforts to the act of persuasion. It is like a client of mine who once rejected a campaign because he thought it would sell too much: 'Tone it down a bit, old chap.'

Generally speaking, agencies do very little promotion of this kind, and when they do it is a matter for extensive soul-searching and discussion. Firstly, they usually indulge in it when the need for new business is at its most critical, and consequently funds are less readily available for the purpose; they are thus extremely nervous about the wisdom of spending the money, displaying through this nervousness a singular lack of faith in their own expertise. Secondly, while agencies are all too ready to offer firm and positive creative recommendations to their clients they make incredibly heavy weather of finding a selling proposition for their own companies. Consequently the material they produce is not representative of their usual creative standards (a point made elsewhere in this book) and fails to generate any real response from prospective clients.

It is very doubtful whether many accounts have ever changed hands as a result of this kind of activity. Clients are far more likely to be impressed by the work done by an agency for other clients, a much better reference point for their opinions; as in many other walks of life, the trumpet plays fewer wrong notes when blown by other people. Agencies can be reasonably objective about their clients, but notoriously subjective about themselves. Any examination of the results of surveys into the methods by which clients select an agency will indicate how little influence agency self-promotion has on the decision.

On the other hand, were it possible (as indeed it is for non-IPA agencies) to make a specific bid for another agency's clients' business, with a full recommendation for creative and media activity, these 'official' promotional methods would change and become more rewarding. Agencies would no longer be inhibited by the necessity for generalisation; they would be able to direct a more positive and relevant proposition to prospective clients selected either because their current advertising was known to be less than effective, or because their existing agency was not doing well. In such circumstances, agencies might be more hopeful of success from the cold canvass method.

The third method – public relations – suffers from not being very precise. It also requires a great deal of patience and not a little expense. A programme of receptions and lunches begins to look like so much wasted effort when the recipients of such generosity later ignore the agency which offers it when they move their accounts. Again, the frustration of the constraints imposed by the Institute are evident: by its nature, a reception given for a dozen marketing or managing directors can only be a very general process of communication, and prospective clients entertained at Epsom on Derby Day are likely to be more interested in the horses or the champagne, or both, than in any thoughts of moving their business.

The same is true of awards to young advertising people offered by some agencies under the pretext of encouraging the development of latent ability or to creative staff for the 'best' advertisement for this or that in a given year. These activities cut little ice with clients, and at the same time compound the introspective attitudes of the industry. In any case, it is fairly true to say that an agency which produces advertisements on the criterion of the likelihood of their winning a prize is concentrating less on the solution of clients' problems than on the superficialities of advertising technique; for the most part, the judges involved in nominating advertisements for these awards have little or no knowledge of the problems the campaigns were originally designed to resolve, and can therefore evaluate them only as examples of abstract creative and mechanical brilliance. The framed accolades hanging on agency walls are thus little evidence of their recipients' advertising sensitivity.

By far the most common method of gaining new business is the cultivation of personal contacts. This has two main advantages: it allows agencies (or, to be more precise, agency executives) to be very specific in the direction of their efforts, and it conveniently avoids the disapproving stare of the IPA. When discussions and negotiations are conducted on this personal level, usually in circumstances of total privacy, it is impossible to say where social pleasantry ends and serious business begins. Such relationships are initiated and developed in a hundred different ways – a chance meeting on the train, a common acquaintance at the club, a dinner party, an advertising conference, or even the renewal of old school, university or service friendships. The germination process can vary in time from a few days to several years, depending on the nature and closeness of the relationship, but the pattern is always similar – the friendly chat, the meetings for drinks or meals, the gradual movement towards discussion of business problems, the invitation to visit the agency, the presentation of the agency's key personnel and carefully selected success stories from the agency's past and current campaigns, more friendly meetings, and finally the opportunity to make a new business presentation on a specific problem, either in competition with other agencies or in isolation.

It is difficult to reconcile this sort of behaviour with the Institute's regulations. In the sense that it can be said to develop 'accidentally' from social activity it presumably avoids falling into the IPA's definition of soliciting; on the other hand, there is no doubt that were it not for the chance it offers of obtaining new accounts much of that social activity would never take place. This is yet a further illustration of the anomalies which exist in the business, and the difficulties it encounters in deciding exactly what its standing is.

On the subject of new business, some comment should be made on the ways in which agencies approach a new business presentation. Most clients, when choosing a new agency, will make a short list of final candidates, usually three. Each of these agencies will be asked to make a presentation on a specified day to show how they would approach the creative and media problems on the account. They may be asked to concentrate on a particular aspect (for example, the creation of a new brand identity or the improvement of a brand's appeal to young people) or the brief may be wide open. In most cases, the agencies will be allowed a fair amount of information about sales and product formulaton, to allow them to adopt a realistic approach to the solution of the client's problem.

Most agencies are only too happy at the prospect of making a new business presentation. Most, indeed, are prepared to go to any lengths to impress a prospective client on such an occasion. Almost all are ready to assemble a vast amount of creative material, the product of a prodigious proportion of the agency's time, effort and money over the days and weeks immediately prior to the presentation, in the hope that the client will be bowled over by the magnificence of the display. A few will be a little more cautious: they will negotiate with the client in advance for a fee to cover presentation costs in the event of their failure to gain the account (if the presentation is successful the fee will be offset against future profits); this fee enables them to perform a more thorough job, since they may well feel that some consumer research is necessary before they can arrive at conclusive creative opinions, and it is usually interpreted by clients as an indication of thoroughness and responsibility.

There are, however, several agencies (all of them large, American and rich) which regard money spent on new business presentations as a capital investment. I have known as much as £5,000 to be spent in this speculative way when it has been by no means certain that the account would be won. Films, recordings, expensive photography, research, computer analysis – all are employed to this purpose. It is not an exaggeration to say that agencies which behave like this are making rods for their own backs; in my experience, clients who are impressed and taken in by these theatrical performances are just as likely, when the account has been handed over and the honeymoon at an end, to move elsewhere on equally fickle grounds, and the agency, which has so recklessly invested its money, to be unable to maintain its lavish impression and to disenchant its client as quickly as it originally wooed him over. Such things are not good for the business; agency and client are equally guilty, and advertising's reputation sinks even lower.

It is understandable, of course, that agencies should be prepared to risk their integrity and reputation in this way: the lure of new business (especially lucrative new business) is a powerful antidote to the falling profits so common in the industry today. There are still some agencies, however, for which the maintenance of basic standards of business behaviour is as important as it is beneficial, and for which the avoidance of the slick and flashy methods of the get-rich-quick (and get-poor-equally-quick) sharp operators is essential to the task of preserving their own self-respect and the admiration of others.

An agency which adopts such an attitude will probably not agree to an *ad hoc* creative presentation to a prospective client; it will prefer to examine the problem it has been given by the client and, after an analysis in depth (either with or without the aid of new research), to suggest to him the broad areas of creative activity which need attention. It will thus be a conceptual exercise, not a theatrical display of creative versality, and it will result from a careful study of all the factors relevant to the problem area. Essentially, the recommendations for future action which will be contained in a presentation of this type will concentrate on the identification of opportunities and the methods of taking advantage of them; no advertisements will be presented. The client will be asked to judge the agency on its ability to evaluate problems, not on its snap creative solutions; the agency's creative work on other accounts provides the evidence of its creativity. In a sense, it is a case of 'take it or leave it', but then a good agency can afford to say this.

The reason for this attitude is clear. No agency with a hard-won reputation wishes to throw it away through a single hasty judgement; advertising campaigns take a long time to devise, and responsible agencies prefer being right in the end to being wrong in a hurry. Hobson Bates is an example of such a company: few new campaigns are thought about in detail until the account is firmly on their books and a great deal of deep and careful analysis has been given to the problem. This shows a proper sense of priorities; far better to devote much analytical thinking to problem definition than to expend excessive creative effort on the attempted solution of a problem which has never been properly defined. In advertising, as in most other activity, a problem recognised for what it is supplies nine-tenths of its own solution.

Agencies like this, which build up the respect and admiration not only of clients and prospective clients but also of other agencies, are less guilty than the rest of them of perpetuating the anomaly of new business acquisition. By and large, the business comes to them of its own accord, convinced by the visible evidence of the agency's excellence. This, however, cannot change the industry's generic fault – its failure to define its own position and its inability to remove its inconsistencies.

Conclusion

Advertising, then, is a business in which anomalies can be seen at every turn. This is not surprising for an industry whose position in the industrial complex is altogether uncertain and difficult to analyse, largely through its own refusal to submit itself to more than a shallow scrutiny.

What this chapter has tried to show is the contradictions and inconsistencies which permeate advertising as a direct result of that mixture of traditionalism, misplaced pride and stubbornness we have called professionalism. It is unfortunately largely due to the influence of its own Institute that advertising is as it is and behaves in the way it does.

There are many people in advertising whose business acumen deserves the highest respect and who are genuine in their devotion to the existing system. These men believe, rightly, that advertising has an indispensable role to play in the marketing process, and perform their tasks with honesty and ability; yet they will disagree strongly with the views expressed here. That is their right. It is, however, probable that they are so concerned with doing immediately what has to be done that they fail to see the shortcomings of their business. This is by no means uncommon, for it is given to very few to stand back from the detail of their environment and see it broadly and objectively.

Perhaps, therefore, before we run the risk of attaching the faults of advertising to all its practitioners, we should say a word of praise to those men and women without whom advertising would be even more culpable than it is. It is through their efforts and diligence that the opportunity exists to build for the business a better future, in which the anomalies we have discussed will disappear.

Chapter 5

Ivory Towers

Introspection

When Alice met the Cheshire Cat in Wonderland she asked it which way she ought to go.[1]

'That depends a good deal on where you want to get to,' said the Cat.

'I don't much care where——' said Alice.

'Then it doesn't matter which way you go,' said the Cat.

'——so long as I get *somewhere*,' Alice added as an explanation.

'Oh, you're sure to do that,' said the Cat, 'if you only walk long enough.'

This delightful piece of Dodgson nonsense contains a basic philosophical principle: that once an objective has been clearly defined the only problem that remains is the means of achieving it. In other words, there has always existed a sharp distinction between the behavioural and physical sciences: physical science may not be able to tell us where to go, but it can certainly tell us the best way of getting there.

All this is by way of a preamble to the theme of this chapter – that most modern advertising agencies are so concerned with the problem of being what they are that they have consistently avoided trying to answer the problem of what they are going to be. They lack, in consequence, any direction or purpose, and concentrate entirely on preserving an existing system which is not necessarily the most suitable either for their clients or themselves. This fixation (that, because the situation now is no different from the situation as it has always been, it will be so in the future) is an extremely dangerous one, for it can lead to an

[1] Lewis Carroll, *Alice in Wonderland* (Dent, 1930), Ch. 6.

increasingly unrealistic relationship between advertising and the rest of industry.

There is no place in modern business practice for conservatism. The only criteria which can be employed to decide where to go and how to get there are those focused on efficiency of operation and fruitfulness of purpose. These criteria will sometimes produce changes in organisation and sometimes changes in operation; they will require people to behave differently and they will result in the adoption of different techniques and formulae. Witness the increased importance of operational research and model building as an aid to decision making, and the almost universal application of computer science.

The developments can of course be abused. A new technique can sometimes become the master of the concept to such an extent that it defeats its own purpose. I recall an instance, when, having carried out the field work for a particular research survey, the research company was asked how quickly the data could be processed: the reply was that the normal period was three weeks (by computer) but tabulation by hand at a premium cost could be provided in five days. Clearly there was some confusion here between the different objectives of cost, speed and convenience.

On another occasion, a major British food manufacturer subjected its advertising media expenditure to an exhaustive operational research examination lasting eighteen months to see whether any reliable formula of correlation between expenditure and sales results could be established. To make the test possible, media schedules were drastically revised at no small risk to the marketing operation, and the testing procedures were organised in the most complex way possible to avoid detection and countering action by competition. The only really certain conclusion that could be based on the results was that in areas where advertising had been significantly reduced there was some reduction in sales level, and in areas where advertising had been significantly increased there was some increase in sales level. There was, however, no precise correlation that could be identified and furthermore no variables were introduced into the analysis to allow for differences of advertisement content or any other influencing factors. The entire exercise was thus of little, if any, value.

Both these examples show the dangers inherent in the pursuit of 'progressive' techniques for their own sake, and indicate the need for a balanced attitude in the compromise between new methods and realistic objectives. Unfortunately, advertising agencies by and large seem to be devoid of any consciousness of the direction of their development and consequently lack the means of achieving it.

Let us take yet another example, this time from an advertising agency, to illustrate this sterile outlook. A year or two ago, at the nadir of the economic depression, when industry was cutting back drastically on its advertising budgets and the smaller agencies were finding it difficult to maintain their existence, one agency whose total billing was in the region of £1million found itself on the horns of a dilemma. Its creative director, an intelligent and able man, had suggested that one way out of the financial difficulty was to form a separate company out of the agency's creative department and to offer specialist design and art services (print, packaging, corporate identity exercises, etc.) while at the same time fulfilling all its normal functions on the agency's contracted accounts. This scheme had the merit of allowing one part of the agency to work on business which might under any alternative arrangement have been turned down either because it was competitive with other accounts or because there was little or no media expenditure involved.

The suggestion was clearly a sensible one, and showed that the creative director was very alive both to the cause and the solution of the problem. The board of directors, however, hesitated; on the one hand, they realised how difficult the financial situation was, but on the other they were conditioned by years of traditional experience and frightened by the possible consequences of change. They therefore did nothing. Their creative director resigned, the agency was shortly swallowed up by a larger company and more than half the staff dismissed. The creative director is now in charge of one of London's most successful creative consultancies.

The fact that such things happen is perhaps less interesting than the reasons why they happen. In Chapter 3 it was hinted that advertising was in danger of protesting too much against a tide of public suspicion through its tendency to retire into its own cosy harbour. This attitude is the result of the inbreeding which has already been described – the desire of advertising to cultivate its own resources and to feed constantly on itself. Any strain which is too closely inbred becomes weak and effete, and after a time suffers from a lack of strengthening blood from another line of breeding. This is what in effect has happened to advertising. Little effort has been made on the part of the industry to seek new blood and broader experience from beyond the confines of its own frontiers, and as a result its own outlook has become more and more restricted and less and less appreciative of the wider problems facing its clients. Perhaps the most revealing way of describing the effect of this attitude is by pointing out that, while the average marketing manager would without undue difficulty be capable of assuming the functions and responsibility of the account executive, most account executives would undoubtedly display considerable evidence of ignorance – particularly in the critically important areas of new product development and product range management – if they were asked to change jobs with their clients.

The single most important reason why this should be is that advertising agencies, which themselves represent a specialist function in the marketing process, have developed to excess the specialisms of their own internal operation. While it is clearly desirable that the different functional areas of advertising should be staffed and controlled by people with expert knowledge in those areas, it is not desirable that such expertise should blinker the expert himself and thus blind him to the importance of other elements in the advertising mix. This is to a very large extent what happens. Specialisation has brought with it its own problems.

In the early days of advertising it was not unusual for one man to write copy, produce a layout, sell it to the client, recommend a media schedule and book the space; he might even, for good measure, produce a type mark-up and order the blocks as well. Such behaviour is shocking to the advertising purists of today: at least seven people would be involved in the modern agency to do the same thing, and they would probably do it better. But they would not do it seven times better, and they might well make the process seven times slower. The old generalists were dedicated and able men, who by taking this broad view of the advertising function were able more easily to perceive the position occupied by advertising in their clients' affairs. They were far more aware, I am sure, than their modern counterparts of the *unity* of advertising activity, of advertising as a single entity rather than a collection of individual skills.

What is more, the men with such an outlook were probably better businessmen, not in the sense that they made more profit out of their business but because they understood what business – in particular their clients' business – was all about. They may not have known the modern science of marketing, but at least they knew the problems with which it is concerned. Far too few people in advertising today know anything about the total marketing process or the profit motive. Consequently, some of the recommendations which they make to their clients are doomed from the start because they fail to appreciate realistically what may or may not be possible financially or operationally in client organisations. This not only represents wasted effort on their part, but it frequently makes them look (and feel) very silly.

It is undeniable that advertising is a specialist part of marketing and only one of many of the marketing manager's preoccupations. It is therefore understandable that advertising people should regard themselves as specialists. Nevertheless, since advertising is responsible for communicating and bringing to life marketing strategy, it is essential that it should do so from a base of knowledge and not ignorance. If agencies are to operate with effectiveness and responsibility they must aim to know as much as they can about marketing as a total business function and its application to their clients' problems in particular.

Too often does it happen that an agency formulates specific media proposals for particular sales or television areas, basing its recommendations on area sales information provided by the client, only to find eventually that its recommendations are totally unrealistic – because it has significantly either under- or over-estimated the costs involved in achieving the sales level indicated by the figures it has been given. Sales figures in themselves, while obviously throwing some light on the relative importance of different sales areas, cannot entirely differentiate accurately between one area and another; consumption *per capita* may vary, competitive activity may not be constant, sales force efficiency may differ according to the geographical disposition of outlets or the density of population, distribution costs may be much higher in one area than another, or the quality of area sales management may be uneven. All these factors can contribute to an extremely wide spectrum of sales costs, and no amount of desk analysis on the part of the agency will identify the root cause of area sales differences if the only information used is that of physical sales revenue.

Most agencies, however, would elect – either for reasons of convenience or because they know no better – to accept without question the information they have been given, with the result that many of their campaigns (or at least the detailed tactics of them) are quite noticeably at variance with their clients' awareness of the true situation. Such indifference to reality is not only irresponsible; it shows only too clearly the limitations of marketing sensitivity in the modern agency.

The truth of the matter is that modern advertising agencies are too concerned with their internal activity to appreciate fully the relevance of that activity to their clients' problems. They adopt a simplistic attitude which seems to want to avoid any chance of being diverted by facts which, though relevant, conflict with their entrenched view. Often I have seen campaigns devised in ten minutes – brilliantly intuitive, superficially admirable; any further market information coming to light after their conception has been ignored or conveniently distorted, with the result that either the client has rejected the proposals out of hand or, if the campaign has been implemented, sales results or penetration research has shown it to have been very inappropriate. Despite the industry's own professed faith in the elimination of risk by advertisement research (see Chapter 2), it is only too ready to rush to creative conclusions before it has entirely satisfied itself as to the true facts. This kind of behaviour has frequently led to client dissatisfaction and, on not a few occasions, to the loss of accounts.

It is not the intention of this chapter to stigmatise all agencies without exception in this respect; there are campaigns (not many, it is true) which have resulted from a total identification by the agency with the client's problem. In these cases the results have normally been successful. But for every campaign so formulated, the same agency will produce half a dozen others which fall short of perfection because it has not for some reason properly done its homework. Perhaps the reason is money: the commission system can play havoc with an agency's sincerity.

The situation would appear to stem from the fact that, in the last analysis, it is the client, and the client only, who is fully competent to appreciate all the facts which may contribute to the overall marketing problem. The agency, no matter how hard it may try and no matter how assiduously it may apply itself to an examination of the facts, can never hope to achieve the proximity of interest that is the client's normal state.

More will be said about this in a later chapter, for it is a point of critical importance in the consideration of future developments in advertising.

It is an irony that at a time when agencies are making less use of their marketing departments than ever before, relegating them almost to the status of a reference library, the advertising industry should need to use them most, if only to keep up with their clients' increasing marketing competence. This confused and confusing situation is a further demonstration of the necessity for some rapid rationalisation of the relationship between advertising and the rest of the business world.

One of the more obvious examples of the inbred self-centredness of the average advertising agency is the 'advertising award', to which a brief reference has already been made in the previous chapter. In principle, there would appear to be little wrong with the practice of acknowledging creative excellence: after all, advertisements can be judged on results only by the agency that produces them or the client who pays for them; other people are not as a rule party to this information. Also, outsiders will by definition base their opinions, not on normal and accepted criteria, but on the less relevant grounds of whether or not an advertisement is clever, pretty or amusing. (We may recall the example quoted earlier of the cinema commercial for a bank's budget account service, which was so funny that its humour completely killed its brand name memorability. As John Hobson said in one of his lectures to the Royal Society of Arts, 'The function of advertising is not to amuse, not to educate, not to pretty the hoardings or enliven the newspapers; it is to sell, and only when the salesmanship is assured can it afford to do the other things as well.') If most people, therefore, are forced through lack of inside information to judge advertising largely on its superficial appeal or its literary or artistic content, who better qualified to do this, it may be asked, than the advertising business itself?

The answer to this question is that the practice leads to misguided attitudes within advertising. Advertising practitioners can too easily fall into bad habits, not the least reprehensible of which is that of slick, hasty and insufficiently substantiated judgement. Worse still, agencies will often (perhaps, it must be allowed, subconsciously) produce advertisements which will attract the attention of their professional colleagues rather more effectively than that of their target audiences. There is thus a great danger that the industry will move away from reality by adopting a language of communication which is fully understood only by itself;

indeed, there are many signs that this is beginning to happen. The language of the consumer is not by and large given over to imagery, poetic hyperbole or the like; it is, more often than not, simple, direct and pragmatic, and it must be questionable whether much of today's advertising speaks in terms which the consumer can readily comprehend, even though it may in principle be saying the right things.

Let us take an example, chosen at random from an edition of the *Radio Times*. It is a full-page colour advertisement for a brand of colour television set: the illustration consists of the set (switched on, showing an action shot of a winter sports scene) from underneath which is peeping a folded document with the word 'guarantee' on it, and the headline reads, 'Anyone crazy enough to give a guarantee like this deserves to have his set examined.' There follows some fairly lengthy copy in three columns, about 375 words, explaining why the manufacturer is able to offer a two-year guarantee on all the set's parts, including the tube, with free service labour during the first year.

It is a good selling proposition, unique in fact. Yet the communication of it is clouded in mystery. Presumably the intention is that the headline, through being intriguing and not immediately intelligible, will make people curious to seek an explanation from the copy; this is crediting the reader with too much patience and interest. The headline is trying to be too clever by half: it is a veiled allusion to the old joke (not all that well known) that anyone who goes to a psychiatrist needs to have his head examined. There can be no doubt that the agency which created it was very pleased with it. Whether it was ever tested in any way is not known, but it is doubtful because it is extremely unlikely that it would have scored highly; what is not in doubt is that a more straightforward statement of the proposition, less tortuous and less open to misinterpretation or incomprehension, would have scored better. It is a perfect instance of advertising talking to itself.

This sort of advertisement could well win an award from one of the many bodies which offer them. Almost every club, association, institute and society (indeed, almost every company even remotely concerned with advertising) invites agencies to submit advertisements as candidates, and the winners are announced in the columns of the trade press with much ceremony; in the case of press advertisements the names of the art director, copywriter, photographer (and sometimes even the block-maker) are noted for posterity, while competitions for cinema or television commercials produce an even larger list of participants – scriptwriter, producer, lighting-cameraman, agency, production company, director, etc. There is almost as much fuss made of the winners at the Cannes or Venice commercial films festivals as there is of a Hollywood Oscar.

All this is very bad for the business. David Ogilvy once said, when giving advice to an advertiser on how to select an advertising agency, that the ones to be avoided were those with an advertising award framed in their reception hall; he also said that he would never allow his own company to submit for such an award. Again, a glance down the list of agencies submitting entries in these competitions will indicate several notable absentees, almost without exception those whose reputation is above such things; but at the same time, some of the best-known names in the advertising agency world will be there.

There are, of course, some agencies which indulge in this sort of behaviour more than others. The symptoms are more obvious to their brother agencies than they are to the outside world. There are even agencies (and it would be invidious, if not actionable, to mention names) which have built a sizeable reputation as a result of this irresponsible policy of producing advertising not on the criterion of its effectiveness in selling their clients' products but on that of its power to woo other clients and attract the attention of other agencies. At least half a dozen major campaigns produced during the past two years fall into this category.

Few, if any, other branches of industry behave like this. The fact that advertising does is thus significant, for it suggests that it sometimes observes motives which are not the motives governing the bulk of industrial action. Certainly, the ultimate objective is that of profit, but at the expense of the responsibilities which advertising bears towards its clients. The ethics of business have given rise to a sizeable bibliography, and the problem has fascinated many behavioural commentators without, it would seem, any great measure of success (the fundamental incompatibility often encountered between individual and corporate priorities, for instance, has never been satisfactorily resolved, though that is not the issue here); the advertising industry would doubtless give these authors much food for thought.

The root cause of this introspective attitude in the agency world lies, I suppose, in that same desire for professionalism described in

Chapter 3. Like many modern artists who paint not for the public but apparently for some inner personal catharsis, advertising seems to assume an arrogance which insists on being judged on another plane from that of the rest of business, a sort of take-it-or-leave-it bravado which is as unrealistic as it is dangerous.

It has been known for an agency to take such a firm stand on its ideas that it will resign an account rather than accept the dictates of its client. This is a rare occurrence, because agencies are not overfond of sacrificing their profits. However, when an issue involving so-called loss of face and the surrender of principles is at stake the characteristics of advertising attitudes tend to blur the considerations of business acumen. In most cases of this kind, the clash of wills is based on causes which are not generally obvious to outsiders; terse announcements in the trade press state merely that such-and-such an agency has found it impossible to agree with such-and-such a client, and that both parties have agreed that it would be mutually to their advantage to part company. These announcements usually hide the real truth: the cause of the divorce may be due to financial arguments or to clashes of personalities, but it looks better in the press if it is all put down to an inability to see eye to eye on professional marketing strategy. The fact that, taken as a whole, clients are more likely to be able to substantiate their marketing outlook than their advertising agents is forgotten or, at best, conveniently overlooked. Furthermore, in situations like this, it is easy for an agency to forget that it is more difficult to gain accounts than to lose them.

There are sometimes genuine reasons for resigning accounts: I have known at least three instances of perfectly justifiable resignations as a result of evidence as to the lack of creditworthiness of clients. But this seldom happens; most agencies go to a great deal of trouble to investigate a prospective client's credit rating before they accept the account, and in any case they are normally insured against any financial failure. Those who are not have only themselves to blame if a client for any reason at all is unable to pay his bills; what is astonishing in such situations is the look of real surprise and offended dignity on the face of the injured party.

Advertising, then, is living in its own ivory tower, preserving and perpetuating its unconscious isolation from the industrial world. While most advertising men will disagree profoundly with this view, it is significant that they find greater comfort from their own kind than they do from their clients. The annual conference of the Advertising Association (not, it should be noted, restricted to delegates from advertising agencies) looks constantly at methods of improving the techniques, but rarely (if ever) considers the structure of advertising. Perhaps a little less time spent on the present, and a little more on the future, might show a better return.

I once listened to a very long paper given by a well-known agency chairman at such a conference. His theme was 'The Development of Advertising Techniques'. It was a competent, if laboured, discourse which dealt fairly fully with the subject. As he sat down I was left with the feeling of something missing, something he should have said but had not. The first question from the audience identified it: 'Where do we go from here? What future developments are we likely to see?' Astonishingly, his answer was that advertising had few further opportunities for development, and that it was impossible to conceive of a better service to industry. It was reminiscent of a late Victorian speaking of the Empire on which the sun never sets, and typifies the attitudes we have examined here.

However, it may be argued that it may not be a bad thing for advertising to be a little removed from reality; after all, it may be claimed, advertising is a creative process which must be allowed a little more latitude than the manufacturing industries; it needs to preserve its independence in order to preserve its integrity, it needs a loose rein to let its imagination run free; and it needs to be stimulated by objectivity. Certainly. At the same time, however, it must not (and should not be allowed to) become removed from reality to such an extent that it begins to forget that it is a business. There should be no incompatibility between industrial objectives and creative strategy.

This chapter so far has questioned the wisdom of advertising's introspection on the grounds that it creates an unrealistic and artificial relationship with the business process. One important aspect of this problem still remains to be discussed, since it is concerned with that essential ingredient of advertising practice, continuity.

In no area is the result of these inward-looking attitudes more evident than in that of planning. It stands to reason that both client and agency are in due course going to face a serious planning problem if the campaigns created by the agency are persistently founded on the limited involvement so commonly encountered in the industry. For on what basis are plans to be made? Planning, by definition, deals with the future, and we have seen that advertising, by and large, is concerned with the present. If an agency (as it habitually does) looks no further ahead than the compaign currently under review, how can this be reconciled with the standard industrial practice of planning for the years to come? There is a fundamental hiatus in the client/agency relationship.

Consider, for example, the modern attitudes of business organisations. Many estimates have been made of the rate at which existing products are replaced and complemented by new product developments, both by companies themselves and by independent observers. These estimates differ in size, but not in their implication, which is that without a concerted and continuous programme of new product introduction most companies will atrophy and eventually die. Generally speaking, there is a fair measure of agreement on the fact that about 50 per cent of the average company's turnover in ten years' time will consist of products which have not yet even been thought of.[1] Industry will therefore concentrate most of its marketing effort on the endless process of product range rationalisation, that is, the maintenance of an optimum balance between too many, too few, old, modified and new products, in order to ensure that it is not only extracting the maximum profit from its existing business but also matching new and different consumer needs with new and different value satisfactions. Only in this way can the future be regarded with any degree of equanimity.

Hence the considerable sums expended each year on research and development, and the important place occupied by the new product group in the companies of the seventies.

Yet what reflection of these attitudes can be found in advertising? Most agencies cannot even boast a new product development department, and those that can are fairly ineffective, choosing to concentrate more on the outward signs – the packaging and presentation – than the concept itself. Again, this is an example of hasty judgement and superficial thinking. Few agency men have any inkling of the significance of new product programmes or the processes involved in their implementation. They are, on the contrary, all too ready to dash off an

[1] This is true more of companies in the high unit volume packaged goods industries than it is of those organisations concerned with industrial high-value products, but the principle is the same. Most industrial products are the result of technology, which constantly produces new opportunities and is therefore a highly competitive field. The risks are thus very high, and while the opportunities for new products may be fewer, the attendant implications are greater.

advertisement without thinking too deeply about the product's performance, its appropriateness for the company or its contribution to profit. Considerations of the place the new product will occupy in plans for the future are of secondary importance.

Consider also return on investment or capital employed. What advertising agency has this in mind when it faces the problem of a new product launch? And can it really do justice to the problem if it ignores such a basic consideration? How many advertising executives are familiar with the concept of discounted cash flow or net present value? Few, if any.

Industry can no longer think in terms of today (or even tomorrow or next month). Unless it has some idea of its planned progress over the next five years it is unlikely to succeed, for its advertising agencies are unlikely to be of very much help.

The point is that advertising is not a separate entity but a vital part of corporate strategy. Successful advertising is produced through a fusion of client and agency attitudes, both aiming for the same goals, both armed with the same information, and both motivated by the same strategic considerations for corporate success. Without this formula, there is no guarantee that good advertising will result; any success will be fortuitous and random.

It is small wonder, therefore, that we see so much bad advertising, and not a little that is utterly appalling, for few, if any, agencies can claim to have attained such a degree of identification with their clients' attitudes and policies. The reason for this is precisely that self-centredness which pervades the advertising industry; by inhibiting longer-term planning and by creating serious communicational gaps between agency and client it results in the kind of advertising which has been referred to earlier in this chapter – clever but sterile, award-winning but not sales-getting, expensive but ineffective (or, at least, not remotely as effective as it should be).

The moral of all this is well illustrated by the story of the agency creative man who had worked long and hard on a particular campaign for a client who was one of those old-established well-known companies with a head office in the City of London. He devised a brilliantly funny strategy which aroused a great deal of enthusiasm in the agency. Everyone eagerly waited the presentation, which was given in the mahogany panelled boardroom of the client's headquarters (in front of the entire board including the chairman) by the man who had written the campaign: he had been chosen to give it because of the enthusiasm he had been able to generate at the agency.

Sure enough, he soon had the usually sombre directors folded up with laughter which throughout the presentation became louder and louder. At last he sat down, feeling pleased and satisfied with his success. The chairman of the board, collecting himself together with difficulty and wiping the tears from his eyes, just managed to speak: 'That was the funniest thing I've seen in years, Mr Brown. Now can you please show us the real campaign?'

This is, of course, an extreme example, but it is true: it proves the points which have been discussed in the previous pages – the inward-looking agency attitude, the campaign written for advertising people, the lack of understanding of client problems and the concentration on ephemeral superficiality. The fact that the client did not recognise the campaign as the real one is sufficient evidence that the agency could not identify itself with the client's business. It is a salutary lesson which delegates to the Advertising Association annual conference would do well to note.

It is not easy to think of any other activity affecting the lives of the public which is guilty of quite the same degree of introspection and isolation. There is some similarity with architects, many of whom seem unaware of even the basic requirements of comfort, but it is an unsatisfactory comparison since the majority are acutely conscious of their responsibility. Similarly, while there may be members of the legal profession who are more concerned with sophistry than the principles of justice, most lawyers are sensitive to the rightness of a cause. The closest parallel is probably to be found in industrial accountancy, where the gathering, arrangement and transmission of financial information, both in words and figures, have become mechanical and to some extent obsolete. As Carl F. Braun, in his powerful little book *Objective Accounting*, says: 'The training of the average accountant binds him to narrow arithmetical conceptions and makes him quite unequal to the dynamic realities and needs of modern industry. It can be fairly said that industrial accountants as a whole have done the world's worst job of communicating.'[1] And again: 'Accounting . . .

[1] Carl F. Braun, *Objective Accounting: A Problem of Communication* (Alhambra: Braun, 1969), p. 16.

becomes sealed against new ideas, new points of view, changing needs. Inbreeding of ideas and methods does its deadly work of isolating the whole accounting setup from the people it is supposed to serve. Reform cannot come from within, and when pressed from without, is necessarily met by complete lack of understanding.'[1]

There are some familiar words and phrases in these quotations: 'unequal to realities', 'inbreeding', 'isolating', 'lack of understanding' – all of them applicable to the malaise in the advertising industry. Not the least remarkable aspect of the comparison is that both advertising agencies and accountants are concerned with the tasks of communication, the one of selling propositions and the other of information about companies; the one communicates with its clients and with a defined target market, the other with executives within the organisation and with parties outside, such as shareholders, bankers, government and the general public. Both should therefore possess more than an average competence to communicate, and both should be endowed with more than an average sensitivity to the changes and developments in the needs of the people to whom they speak. Neither, it seems, is the case.

Why the parallel should be so close is not obvious. Unless it is pure coincidence, there must be some unknown common characteristic in both kinds of practitioner which leads each of them into a pattern of behaviour totally isolated from outside forces and motivated by nothing other than tradition and irrelevant precedent. Just as the pence are more important to most accountants than the pounds, so to most advertising agencies the rules are more important than the game.

As will be seen in a later chapter, these comments do not necessarily refer to advertising as a whole. It will be observed that several significant developments are taking place which encourage one to feel that there are at least some elements in the industry which are not unaware of the dangers into which advertising is falling; they are prepared to take action both to prevent it and to protect themselves. It is the agencies, changeless and unimaginative, which are being criticised, and it is the advertising agency concept which is the root cause of the trouble – a concept which has very little greater relevance to the advertising needs of modern industry than steam engines have to today's railways. The remedy will lie in the eventual removal of the advertising agency from

[1] ibid., pp. 72–3.

the business scene, for it is impossible to change or modify it. When a suit has been badly cut, it is better to get a new suit than to attempt to have it altered.

The central problem, therefore, is that there is no apparent sympathy between advertising and the rest of the industry. There is no common scheme, no central objective, which the two can accept and recognise as being equally relevant. If the question were one of the relationship between a solicitor and his client, or of a house agent advising a buyer on the virtues of a house, or of a stockbroker recommending a share, the two parties would be under few illusions about their respective interests; as it is, the considerations affecting the agency may not (and, quite probably, will not) coincide with those affecting the client. There is nothing under the present arrangement which makes for a solid and permanent relationship, nothing which encourages industry to think any better of advertising than it has ever done, nothing which would prevent a client – were the alternative to be offered – from adopting a *modus operandi* that is simpler, more direct and less expensive. There is nothing, in other words, to stop industry allowing progress to take its course.

Future Indefinite

From where is the remedy to come? How is the solution to be found? Who is to be the catalyst of this fearful impasse?

Certainly not the advertising agencies – that is, certainly not the people who choose to remain in the agencies. It is precisely because they choose to remain that they are unlikely to recognise the need for change in a situation with which they are themselves so closely and personally identified. The agency to them is an oasis in the middle of an industrial desert, but they do not yet know that the drinking wells are drying up. There is comfort in the protection and shelter of their other world, insulated from reality and the forces of business change.

It is interesting to examine the way in which some of these agency people see the future of the industry. Of all the views I have heard expressed, there is not one which does not assume that the agency will form the basis of any new developments (if that is the proper word): if their views are to be accepted, the future will merely compound the faults of the present. One commonly held opinion is that agencies will continue to grow larger in size and smaller in number, so that eventually

British advertising will be handled by a few large units, competing with each other for business and offering more or less identical standards of service. This seems to ignore two considerations: one is the developments which are already taking place in other directions, which will be referred to in the next chapter, and the second is the need which will still exist for something other than a large advertising agency, particularly from smaller advertisers with modest budgets and companies requiring a special kind of technical knowledge on the part of their creative advisers.

Another view stresses the movement which will take place towards the growing internationalism of business. This will be reflected (indeed, is already reflected) in the emergence of world-wide advertising agencies, particularly those which are US owned. There will be an increasing 'sameness' about advertising for the same product in different countries – drinks, petrol, cars, cigarettes, toiletries. No doubt this is true, but the real reason is not the internationalism of advertising agencies, but the internationalism of advertisers; many international advertising campaigns are handled in different parts of the world by agencies which have no connection with each other whatsoever, apart from the fact that they are working for the same international client. This client-based outlook will be shown to be highly significant for the advertising of the future when we examine it in closer detail.

A third view – clearly based on a failure to appreciate the changing balance of the relationship between advertising agencies and industry – is that the agency almost by definition has a contribution to make across the entire marketing spectrum. This is a left-over from the days (described in Chapter 1) when the early agency marketing departments of the fifties were generally speaking better equipped than their client counterparts. Times, as we have seen, have changed, but this has largely gone unnoticed; while, in setting up those departments, the agencies have been unjustly criticised by recent commentators [1] as having 'had more money than sense', there is no doubt that they helped to stimulate the development of similar attitudes amongst their clients which have in turn rendered this aspect of agency service redundant. To imagine that an agency still possesses a superior marketing competence is both unrealistic and out of date, and the fact that the view

[1] *The Financial Times*, 'Agencies Take a Back Seat', 27 April 1972.

is still to be found indicates the degree to which advertising has been blind to the new environment. Furthermore, agency people clearly feel that this marketing responsibility, far from having already ended its useful life, will continue indefinitely into the future; this is more than unrealism, it is pure fantasy and self-delusion.

Current attitudes, therefore, either fail to recognise the extent to which industry has changed over the last few years, or assume without real justification that no changes in advertising can take place which are not consistent with the continuation of the advertising agency as the basic unit of the business.

This invests the agency with a sacrosanctity to which it should never presume. It is by no means axiomatic that what has served for 130 years will continue to serve indefinitely, and there is a kind of arrogance about advertising's opinion of itself which is unattractive and unjustified.

There must necessarily be new thoughts given to the future, thoughts which can begin, not by asking the question 'How will the advertising agency best serve the needs of industry?' but by seeking to discover a total structure of advertising which will provide the type of service that clients require, and at the same time will use the undoubted skills which exist in today's agencies to better effect by releasing them from the inhibitions and constraints which have been described. Furthermore, there must be acceptance of the fact that it is the customer – the client – who is the best judge of what he needs, since only he knows the kind of relationship which most satisfactorily complements his own strengths and weaknesses.

In short, it is not so much the expertise which is at fault in modern advertising, but the framework of the structure within which it is exercised. The structure of the advertising agencies is the cause of most, if not all, of the industry's shortcomings, not only in terms of the way it works but also in terms of the attitudes which emanate from its practitioners. Removed from its straitjacket, it would be at once both more efficient and more economic. All the weaknesses we have discussed – the aping of the professions, the commission system, the duplication of effort, and so on – stem largely from the fact that there is a basic inflexibility in the average agency which inhibits change and perpetuates inefficiency. What is worse, these weaknesses and this inflexibility are defended by agency people because to do otherwise would be tantamount to an admission of the inappropriateness of the agency itself. What these people fail to realise is that by defending these shortcomings they do little to improve the image of the industry.

We have to begin, therefore, by identifying the elements in the business which are most likely to stimulate the kind of new thinking that has been described. The previous chapter closed with a reference to those advertising people who are at last beginning to realise the dangers and the limitations of the traditional system, and who through their efforts and imagination are forming the nucleus of a new style of advertising service. Whether most of them realise the full significance of their actions it is hard to say, but there can be no doubt that it will be from what they have started that the real steps forward will be made. It is important to realise that no major change can be made from within the agencies: their structure is such that they cannot perform their function without a strict adherence to the financial and organisational rules by which they are bound. Thus it will inevitably be those people seeking methods and opportunities outside the agencies who will gain the freedom of movement with which to succeed.

Next, what kind of people will these be? Is it possible to say with any certainty which functional areas of the agencies will provide these pioneers? From the evidence we have, it seems that it is precisely those areas which are valued most by clients that will realise their own importance. For example, it is extremely unlikely that industry is going to weep bitter tears at the disappearance or unavailability of account executives: what these people can do, industry can do better. Indeed, if we examine the functions and responsibilities of the account service man, as explained in Chapter 2, we can see that he has to a large extent been made superfluous by the advance of marketing expertise within client organisations. His experience is duplicated by the skills and resources which exist in almost every industrial concern, and in nearly all cases improved upon and intensified. In short, he is a man developed and perfected by the agencies to perform a function peculiar to themselves; he is irrelevant, through his shortcomings, to the average business. What he will do, if the agency disappears, is a sobering and perplexing thought, though it is doubtful whether his loss will be a source of great sorrow. He clearly has a role within the advertising agency, but it is artificial in a wider context, born as it is from a system which is no longer appropriate to modern requirements. The long-vaunted picture of the smart, slick young advertising man is fading into the mists of the past; he once had a part to play, but his usefulness is rapidly coming to an end.

The account executive, therefore, will not be in the vanguard of the revolution. He has no proposition to offer which will attract his clients to a new dimension of advertising. Who then? Will it be the media man, who has over the years cultivated a peculiarly specialised science, hedged around with readership analyses, cost per thousand calculations and duplication figures? The man whose expertise can smooth out the differences between a budget of £200,000 and a budget of £300,000 by skilful and experienced planning and buying? The man who is at the very centre of the negotiating machine, who links client with supplier, who spends the money the client provides?

It is improbable, because for all the media man's qualities, for all his skill and technical experience, there are two factors which militate against it. Firstly, he is not, in the true sense of the term, an advertising man; he is a technician, schooled in the facts and figures of newspaper and television audiences. He may understand and be able to articulate on the quality of these figures; he may even at times display some creative imagination – far beyond the capabilities of his computer – which will inspire a client to spend more and with greater success – but he is not a communicator, and he does not easily understand the language of communication.

Secondly, because the media man is what he is, he is reproducible. Given the time and opportunity and money, a client can make one of his own. It is not particularly important that a media man works for an advertising agency; the fact that in doing so he earns a commission for his employer is irrelevant – the media owners are sensible enough not to turn down revenue if it is big enough, no matter where it comes from, and commissions are built into their rate structures. It is thus merely as a by-product of the agency system that the science of media analysis has grown up, and it is only because the system does not allow for clients who perform their own media planning that such people have in the past been found exclusively inside the agencies; but this is changing, as we shall see. Since they are at the centre of the system, they are unlikely to be the first to change it.

Thus we have examined two of the three major components of the agency, and found that they are too intrinsically involved to assume the responsibility for change. Before considering the third – the creative element – we may briefly examine the 'service' functions. Print we can discard immediately – it makes little profit for the agency and is little used by clients because of its expense. Agency print men are hardly the prophets of change. Production men, also, exist in agencies because the system demands that they do: they are necessary to implement the work created by other people – to provide the means of reproducing it in its millions and putting it before the public. As for agency marketing men, all that can be said is that the best of them have long since moved over to client companies, in the absence of any stimulation from advertising. Those that are left can hardly be considered as revolutionaries. Finally, market research is already a separate function; agencies who are seriously involved in this service have formed separate companies for the purpose – Marplan and Interscan are examples – and the rest maintain a research department merely as an extension of outside research organisations, acting as a kind of broker for the agency's clients.

We are thus left with the creative element of advertising, the hub upon which advertising revolves. Advertising agencies are judged largely on their creative output; it is the one really visible piece of evidence which can be evaluated without visiting the agency or talking to its management. (The fact that it is frequently evaluated wrongly is immaterial; nothing will obstruct the course of subjective opinion.) It is therefore not surprising that creative people are more sensitive to the attitudes of others than their colleagues elsewhere in the agency, and more conscious of the need to be – and to be seen to be – successful.

Within the environment of the typical advertising agency, creative people frequently find that their freedom of thought is the slave of operational expedience. The encumbrances of the traditional client/agency relationship often limit the opportunity which may exist. True, many creative people are wayward and undisciplined in their thinking, unable to keep to the central purpose of a problem and needing much careful control and direction; but there are many others who, given their head, can not only inject into a chosen strategy life, vigour and powerful communication but also go most of the way towards supplying the strategy itself through their innate appreciation of the needs of the situation. Such men and women clearly experience many frustrations in their agency work, and the fact that in many agencies creative people are kept very much behind the scenes for client presentations makes matters worse; clients often want to see and talk to the writer or the art director who is responsible for creating their campaigns (certainly most creative people like to meet clients, if only to be sure that their work is not being misrepresented), but the conservative attitude of agency account management frequently prevents this.

This state of affairs is difficult to understand. On the one hand, it is creative performance which earns an agency its reputation; on the other, in nine agencies out of ten the people who achieve that performance play second fiddle to the administrators, being forced to follow an unpalatable strategy and unable to get close to clients.

If changes are to be made, then, it is going to be the creative people who instigate them. In the first place, despite the scant respect meted out to such people in many agencies, modern advertising now depends more on its creative competence than on any of its other services; where marketing was once the hall-mark of a respectable agency, the emphasis is now very firmly on words and pictures. In the second place, creative people are beginning to realise their importance and – what is more – to discover that their performance is in no way impaired by the absence of agency trappings.

While it is through creativity that advertising will escape from the stifling vapours which afflict it (the anomalies and inconsistencies we have examined), it is questonable whether it is from any deep-rooted recognition of these anomalies that the rebels will protest; they are likely to be far more concerned with the discovery of greater opportunities of their own self-fulfilment. Nevertheless, the seizure of these opportunities will carry with it the almost accidental foundation of a totally new structure of the industry, and the removal of most of the problems which beset the agencies of today.

There is a new spirit of adventure and experimentation running through agency creative groups, a spirit which can find no expression inside the boundaries of organised advertising. Some very well-known names in the creative world have already appeared on the platform of change, and many more will follow. Nor do they lack encouragement from the people who matter, the clients who foot the advertising bill; many of our largest companies have already shown themselves willing to join in this experiment, doubtless because of their own disenchantment with the current arrangement and their desire to establish something more germane to their needs.

Instinct might indicate that the change will be permanent, but it requires more than this to convince the entrenched traditionalism of the agencies. If more evidence is needed, let the clients speak for themselves. One well-respected industrialist told me recently that he would be much happier with his advertising if it were not for his advertising agency; another confessed that he was sure there must be easier ways of achieving the campaigns he ran; and yet a third complained that if his advertising agents paid as much attention to his company's publicity problem as they did to the choice of carpet in their reception hall he would be more than happy. The truth is clearly that the machine is running the operator.

Such comments are not often heard, it is true; but when they are made they come from the heart, and express without question the unspoken feelings of the many clients who have long ago resigned themselves to a long-suffering acceptance of a situation which seems incurable. This is why, if all the people who now work in advertising agencies were to ignore the consequences of stagnation and were to attempt to perpetuate the situation which is so cruelly shouting out for change, the prospect would be painfully bleak. Mercifully there are those amongst them who can see the light, who can recognise the problem and who have the will and the courage to tackle it.

To this chosen few are given the responsibility and the reward for changing the face of British advertising. Historically, the change will be more important than any other. No longer is the path ahead merely choked with undergrowth and dipping branches: it has disappeared completely and a new trail must be blazed. Whether the new road will travel in the right direction for other countries is not for this book to say; there is evidence to suggest that advertising in both the USA and the rest of Europe is not so precariously poised, since it is spared many of the artificial constraints which pervade our own. What is certain is that, when British advertising has recovered from its change of life, other countries will peer at it with a new and keener interest, in the hope of reaping some benefit from their scrutiny.

It cannot be stressed too much that the metamorphosis we shall see will strike at the very roots of the industry; indeed it will do so to such an extent that advertising will to all intents and purposes become another industry altogether. If so, it may be argued that when the structure crumbles it will drag down with it all the safeguards and protective mechanisms which exist to limit the misuse of its power, and that there will therefore be no longer any guarantee that it is honest and truthful.

This is not so. All these safeguards are independent of advertising. The exercise of them is largely in the hands of media owners or government authority. There is therefore no reason to suppose that advertising produced by a different process will be any more or less reprehensible than it is today. It is precisely because of advertising's present structure that the forces of control have been imposed from without; if this structure disappears, and advertising becomes more an intrinsic part of the total industrial complex, not a separate estate as it is now, it could well be maintained that it will be more closely identifying itself with the interests of both client and consumer. It will be more ready to understand the requirements of each.

Such, then, are the needs of future advertising. If the needs are ignored, the only alternative is a slow detrition of the industry's authority and respect. This chapter has tried to show that not only does the opportunity for improvement exist, but that also there is in advertising today the means of taking advantage of it. Indeed, the process has already begun, and it will be the purpose of the next chapter to explain in detail how the transition is being made from an outmoded and unwieldy complex to an efficient and relevant service, geared fully to the demands placed upon it by industry.

As will be seen, this new concept will grow logically and steadily from what exists today, preserving the good and casting aside the bad; it will be cheaper, simpler and more efficient; it will satisfy clients and its own practitioners alike; it will perform its own specific function without unnecessary duplication of effort; and, finally, it will be equipped to expand with the growth of the clients it will serve.

PART III

Chapter 6

The Winds of Change

The Product/Market Match

One of the basic tenets of the marketing concept is that known as 'matching the product to the market'.

Marketing is essentially a customer-orientated process, which requires that the sale of a product or a service is the result of your providing the buyer with what he wants, not of finding a buyer for something you have. While to many people in industry these may be one and the same thing, there is in fact a world of difference between them. The difference lies in the reason for the existence of your product or service: in a company which adopts a true marketing philosophy, no product or service will be developed unless the need for that product or service has been previously identified through research or observation, and unless the likely demand for it can be located and quantified in advance. Thus the product, when made, can properly be said to 'match the market'.

The alternative is to make the product and then to look for customers for it. This is a hazardous operation, carrying with it a very high failure risk and frequently resulting in a 'product/market mismatch'.

In a situation where the product is accurately matched to a market need, the function of selling is not onerous. In a situation where it is not known whether or not the product is accurately matched to a market need, the function of selling can be very difficult and frequently impossible.

If we examine the modern advertising agency in these terms, we might justifiably expect to find the marketing concept being applied, bearing in mind that advertising is one of the critical ingredients in the marketing mix. Our examination will show, however, that this is not the case; on the contrary, there is a weight of evidence to indicate that what clients want and what the agency is offering are by no means the same thing. There is, in effect, in the modern British advertising industry a clear example of product/market mismatch.

In order to show how this happens, it is interesting to compare two things: firstly, we must examine what industry is seeking from its advertising agencies, and secondly, we must see how the agencies describe themselves to the outside world through their own promotional activity.

In Chapter 4 it was pointed out that in today's industrial and economic environment, companies have developed a competence in all the skills normally performed by the advertising agency with the notable exception of creative expertise. Every other function – research, marketing, print and even media – can be satisfactorily reproduced by the client himself. It has been shown that, while there may be a place in client organisations for most of the advertising functions, there is a very strong case to be advanced for the maintenance of a totally separate and independent creative service, which can bring to bear on a problem objectivity, freshness and imagination uncoloured by the proprietary interest which distorts many management decisions.

Again, reference has been made to the many surveys designed to shed light on a client's decision to appoint a new advertising agency. In every case, the paramount requirement is that an agency should be creatively outstanding; no other attributes, no matter how impressive, will attract new business if the agency cannot prove its creative ability. In this respect, it should be remembered that nine out of ten decisions on the appointment of a new agency are made on the evidence of that agency's previous work for other clients and products, as illustrated by the advertisements it has produced.

The next requirement indicated by these surveys, in order of importance, is that of efficient service. This can be shown in many ways (indeed, in a sense it may be argued that a high standard of creative work represents good service, since it avoids time wasted on second attempts at the same problem): speed, accuracy, honesty and interest all manifest the attribute, but at bottom it stems from a fundamental desire to be thoroughly involved in clients' problems.

How strange, therefore, when an agency sets out to devise its own selling proposition, and to encapsulate in an advertisement or a broadsheet what it believes to be its main attraction, that it should concentrate so much on what appears to be at total variance with the requirements pinpointed by the surveys. Take, for example, the following claims put forward by agencies in recent advertisements, and chosen at random:

Always leading the field in latest marketing techniques.

. . . total marketing operation.

The key to modern marketing.

A complete marketing service.

Identification of marketing problems.

Much more for your money.

and, very ominously,

Tomorrow's advertising agencies will look . . . like we look today.

Out of these seven claims, five concentrate on the marketing ability of the agencies concerned, not one mentions creative ability and not one mentions service; yet all of these agencies must have seen the results of the surveys mentioned earlier. Not one has thought fit to stress the things clients want most.

Clearly, what has happened in these examples is that either the agencies concerned have failed to appreciate what it is that the market needs and demands, or they are labouring under the delusion that industry, when looking for a new agency, is still seeking the qualities which were required twenty years ago. In either event, the product does not match the market. Small wonder, therefore, that some agencies find the task of attracting new business so formidable; and what an irony that they should use marketing competence as the cornerstone of such misguided claims! Clients can hardly be blamed for passing quickly by such a patent example of what Theodore Levitt would call 'marketing myopia'.[1]

The other side of this particular coin is that creative service, in addition to representing the quality most sought after by prospective clients, also happens to be what the agencies can do best. An agency's account service personnel could quite easily, save for some accident of life, have chosen to devote themselves to almost any other non-technical

[1] Theodore Levitt, 'Marketing Myopia', *Harvard Business Review*, July–August 1960.

management function elsewhere in industry. (They may possibly have chosen advertising because it looked a congenial occupation, but they were certainly not born to it.) The same is true of agency marketing staff; most of the best have already moved over to industry in any case. As for media men, the peculiar combination of attributes which manifests itself in their skills could conceivably have been directed towards some other walk of life such as finance or insurance or market research. Creative people, on the other hand, choose to be what they are because they would not be happy doing anything else; they may have gravitated towards journalism, but they are unlikely to be found elsewhere in industry. Advertising, combining as it does the artistic and the commercial, is the ideal outlet for their talents.

Thus, the advertising agencies have what in their own language is called a 'product plus'. Their specific skill is the creation of sales propositions, which is exactly what clients find they need most because they lack the resources of their own to provide it. Yet, despite this perfect match, the agencies appear to be ignoring the opportunity.

Crumbling Structures

In the previous chapter it was argued that changes in the structure of the advertising industry are both necessary and inevitable, and that these changes would be instigated by creative people. It can be seen from the previous section how critical creative competence is to an agency and consequently what a strong and influential position creative people occupy.

The traditional structure of advertising is already showing signs of incipient collapse. True, the edifice will stand for a few years yet, but the rot is in the foundations, and there is a limit to the length of the time that they can continue to support what is above them. Let us therefore examine in detail how these changes are coming about.

The single most important aspect of the transformation is the development of creative consultancies. These are quite separate from the agencies, and are being formed at a fast pace by agency creative men and women who are not only disenchanted by the conditions which have been described but also recognise the opportunities which exist in an independent unit. Sometimes labelled 'hot shops' by the agencies they have forsaken, they are concentrating singlemindedly on the provision of a straight creative service to industry. Their terms of reference are quite simple: to give clients what they want

The people who are branching out into this relatively new venture are amongst the best creative brains in advertising. They are drawn from both the literary and artistic side of advertising. They have clearly decided that if clients wish their creative work to be an intrinsic part of their own marketing planning, it is only through the close involvement of personal interest; these people are very personally involved with clients – they accept their brief unquestioningly and provide the best possible interpretation of that brief, uncluttered and untrammelled by any other distractions. Their service to the client is total within their specific terms of reference: they perform the task to the absolute limits of their skill. They are unconcerned with media planning, with marketing strategies, or with the search for information; their function is purely creative, and the quality of that function is conditioned only by the extent of the client's own marketing knowledge, an area upon which they steadfastly refuse to tread.

It may be interesting to quote examples. One agency art director, who knew his job well but failed to see eye to eye with the managing director (who felt that his own marketing skill exceeded that of the client) was finally forced into the position of having to resign. The situation was made more distasteful because he was an old personal friend of the managing director and had served him well, but this made no difference; they had even been partners together in a previous agency. When his period of notice expired, he had still not found a new job. He was offered occasional freelance work, which he of course accepted but did not regard as very important. Eventually, however, the freelance work increased, and he realised that it was doing so because of his personal relationship with the clients for whom he was producing it. The clients, all of whom employed advertising agencies, for their part discovered that they were able for once to discuss on a really personal level the problems which their advertising posed, and were coming to him to explore not only the peripheral details of advertising – packaging, label designs, exhibition stands, etc. – but more and more the central creative proposition, the platform on which their whole campaign was based.

It took some time for the reality of the situation to become clear; indeed, it was not until the art director realised that the income from his freelance work was assuming proportions greater than his previous salary that the truth emerged. He was, he discovered, beating the agencies at their own game; he had no contractual commitment, he had no bureaucratic management structure, he was in no way beholden to media owners, and he was in complete command of his own enterprise. What is more, he had a number of extremely satisfied clients, some of whom were even insisting that their own advertising agencies immediately incorporate into their campaigns the ideas which he himself had formulated and developed. Bewildered but nevertheless gratified, he took the decision to register his own company, as a design and advertising consultant, and is now better off than he has ever been in his whole life. He has a staff of five, and his annual turnover produces a profit equal to that of an agency with a payroll of forty and billings of at least £$\frac{3}{4}$ million.

Another creative man, this time an agency copywriter (strangely enough, from the same agency), decided that he was not as a general rule being given the opportunity to exercise his abilities to the full within the confines of the organisational structure in which he worked. He therefore decided to set up his own creative workshop in the hope that his reputation would attract work from clients for whom he had in the past produced campaigns. He was not disappointed. Even before he had finally parted company from the agency, he was approached by his employer's own clients with requests to examine their creative problems and to recommend on broad areas of creative activity. These projects were almost invariably concerned with the formulation of basic creative concepts, the fundamental proposition around which advertising campaigns are built.

This is an important example, because it illustrates one of the main reasons why these new units are attractive to industry. Clients are generally competent to handle the mechanics of advertising, the technical and quantifiable aspects of this traditionally artistic function; what they are not competent to handle is the one element which gives it life, the 'brightness' to flavour the 'rightness' (in John Hobson's terms). They are even able to translate and expand the concept once it has been devised, but they cannot contrive the initial spark to kindle the flame.

Once again, one of the more significant points to be observed in this example is the fact that the market for this kind of service is exactly the same as that for the traditional agency; indeed, since clients used the service for their basic creative requirements, it suggests either that they were already dissatisfied with what they had or that the new opportunity was immediately recognised as a better proposition. In any event, it was clearly more suitable to the purpose.

There is a further aspect of this new movement which can be illustrated by a third example. For want of a better term this will be called the 'desire for a corporate identity'. All advertising campaigns are a function of the marketing process, but they are at the same time a part of that total communication between company and customer, between industry and the outside world. This communication operates at many levels: it can be observed in the correspondence from the company to its customers, suppliers and the public; it can be seen in the design of its transport fleet; it is evident in the packaging of its products; it is shown on the many pieces of display material at the point of sale; it is frequently present in the product itself. Any visible or tangible element in the relationship between the company and the society in which it operates is an opportunity to be seized for the strengthening of the company's total corporate identity or image. Advertising is one of the greatest of these opportunities, and, as such, one of critical importance in the building of that image.

It is not surprising, therefore, that the third example of the forces of transformation should come from the ranks of those creative people who have taken this catholic view of the communication process, reaching beyond the borders of advertising itself and seeking to find expression in the totality of relationships between their clients and society. The man in question was by training a commercial artist, but he had, over the years, progressed from mere visualisation and illustration through art direction to the function of creative director, the person responsible for the conception of creative platforms and central selling propositions. His whole career had been spent in the agency world.

Like so many others in his situation, the break with the agency stemmed from a fundamental revolt against the strictures of advertising bureaucracy. He was unwilling to be restrained and confined to the narrow limits of the creative briefs with which he frequently disagreed, and therefore decided to go his own way. In establishing his own business, it mattered little to him at what point he became involved with his clients' problems, as long as it was a point on the circumference of the communication circle. In some cases, he was asked to produce a new pack design; in others, he was commissioned to supply new letter-headings, business cards or leaflets; occasionally he was given the task of solving the total corporate identity problem; but – and this is significant – he was rarely asked to produce an advertising campaign as his first responsibility. This last was invariably the logical outcome of his other efforts.

He is now enjoying great success; and the reason for his success is that he has realised the nature of industry's need. He is not so much concerned with a client's marketing policy (although of course he needs to understand it and identify his work with it in order to produce sympathetic creative ideas) as he is with the problem of turning his creativity to the service of the client's total business objective. In this way, in all he does he is performing a function which he can perform infinitely better than the client himself, in marked contrast to the advertising agency whose operations represent so much duplication of the work of the companies it serves.

These new departures are based on a happy disregard of the rules of the game. The evidence they display of a desire to get on with the job indicates the frustration and impatience which such people suffered in the agency world. They have established an entirely new concept of creative service as a result and given the lead to the long-needed reform of the industry.

The economics of the exercise are interesting, too. The staff required to perform this service is very small indeed compared with the numbers involved in an agency, and, since there can be no question of a commission system in the absence of media expenditure, all work is carried out on a fee basis. Yet clients who already employ agencies (from whom creative work is free, or rather paid for out of commission) are willing to pay these fees; which speaks well of the standard of the work provided. Indeed, because there exists no contractual arrangement between the consultant and his client it is the standard of the work alone which preserves the relationship.

It is not only creative people, however, who have made the move, although in their case the reasons are more obvious. Other elements of advertising have for a long time been murmuring in protest. The pattern has generally been one of a movement away from specialisation within the agency to specialisation by specialist units. Take, for example, merchandising; this below-the-line activity has developed with the increase in importance of the retail middleman, who has during the last ten years assumed a value in the chain of distribution far in excess of his previous status. In the old days, a retailer depended on the strength of the national manufacturer for his livelihood: the manufacturer supplied the product, provided a promotional campaign for it and sold it to the retailer in anticipation of the demand which he hoped had been stimulated. Usually it worked, and the retailer took his promised profit.

These days things are very different. The retailer is in a position of enormous strength; with the proliferation of products in almost every field, and the concomitant increase in competition for shelf space in the supermarkets and self-service stores of the modern high street, manufacturers are finding that it is not enough merely to provide national advertising support for their products. Now they need to do far more: they need both to 'push' and to 'pull' their products through the retail channels. In addition to the help of advertising they have to exert other pressures to get their product *into* as well as *out of* the shops; they have two selling jobs to do – they have to sell *to* the trade and they have to sell *for* the trade.

Consequently, below-the-line merchandising activity has in recent years accounted for an increasing proportion of client budgets, a trend which has been accelerated by the economic conditions that depressed industry in 1968 and 1969. The agencies, by and large, did not take advantage of this new opportunity; indeed, in many ways they resisted it. Their attitude was compounded of a mixture of typical conservatism and blind devotion to the commission system; these new merchandising expenditures carried no commission apart from the incidental campaigns which were sometimes mounted in support of a particular promotional exercise, and thus the agencies left the major responsibility for planning such activity mainly in the hands of their clients.

There were two results of this. Firstly, although a few agencies did try to become involved in providing a merchandising service, it was not comprehensive enough and left the client with the responsibility for implementing and controlling the plans they submitted. One agency (internationally well known) confesses that it was not interested in such affairs and was glad to get rid of the tiresome obligation to do something.

Thus clients were left holding the baby, and were forced by necessity to do the work themselves.

This necessity was mother to the second result. Those agency people who were peripherally involved in merchandising were frustrated both by the apparent lack of importance attached to it by their employers and by the sight of their clients directing more and more attention to these operations. They recognised the opportunities which existed in this field and decided to take advantage of them. Within a very short time, many of them had left the agencies and set up organisations specifically designed to relieve industry of this burden and to plan, implement and control sales promotion schemes from start to finish.

In this way, the functions of the agencies were fragmenting even further. These 'promotion agencies' (as they began to be called) had at one blow severed a large slice of potential profit from organised advertising; once again, it was a case of offering the client what he wanted. Furthermore, what must be particularly galling to advertising agencies is that whenever a promotion takes place they have, as often as not, to work in close co-operation with these new units to whom they have so prodigally surrendered the initiative. Merchandising services are now an industry in themselves, and cover all types of promotion schemes. Perhaps the area in which they are most often involved is that of premium offers (free or reduced-price items linked to the purchase of the client's product), which are purchased in staggering quantities, sometimes from manufacturers whose entire production is devoted to this market. (Incidentally, it is worth pointing out here that certain modifications to this type of activity may be necessary now that Britain has officially joined the EEC, since most European countries have very strict regulations governing the sale of reduced-price goods.)

Within the relatively short time that they have been in existence, these new organisations have brought many innovations into promotional schemes. The most notable is the development of sport as a selling tool, traditionally the preserve of public relations. Not content with the availability of prominent sportsmen and sportswomen to recommend and give testimonials for products (a practice which has been common enough for a long time) nor with opportunities open to clients for the sponsorship of sporting events (golf tournaments, show jumping, etc.), they have taken the exploitation of sporting figures to even greater lengths. Medallions, photographs, competitions, autographed products and an extension of sponsorship to football, tennis, cricket and rugby league have all proliferated along with the growth in professional sport and the birth of a new breed of sports 'agents' who reap a formidable commercial profit out of their protégés. The zenith of such activity was reached in 1970 when the entire England World Cup team gave its name to a long list of products and promotions organised jointly by a merchandising company and a sports agent.

The strength of these new units is, like that of the creative consultancies, their personal service and the specific nature of the function they perform. Here also there are the same clear-cut terms of reference; there is no confusion over the degree of involvement and no question of duplication of effort. The service is paid for partly by fee and partly by any profit made on the supply of premium items.

In addition to the departure of creative and sales promotional personnel from the formal agency structure, a word needs to be said about the position of media men in this new type of advertising service. Traditionally, media men have been a focal point of the advertising scene since the beginning; they are in a sense the nucleus of the business for, apart from the creative service which is the major client requirement, it is the media function which provides the financial foundation without which no agency could stand. Commissions received by the agency from media owners in return for space or air-time bookings are the lifeblood of modern advertising; after all, it was primarily as a booking agency that the service appealed to clients at the very outset.

It may be asked, therefore, whether the agency can maintain its existence purely as a media planning and buying organisation when its creative service is being usurped by independent consultancies. In a way, the question is an unreal one, since if the agency is stripped of its other functions it no longer merits the description of an advertising agency in the accepted sense of the word. There are, however, two points to be made.

The first has already been discussed in Chapter 4: the media function is clearly becoming less of an agency prerogative with the increasing ability of manufacturers not only to develop their relationships with the media themselves but also to conduct their own planning and buying of media schedules. It has been shown that many of our larger companies are taking it upon themselves to analyse and evaluate the problems which face them in the complex and well-documented media situation of today; a modicum of experience, a logical mind and a slide rule (or at best a computer) are really the only tools required in this particular trade; that other attribute – the ability to sign a large lunch bill – is unnecessary, since the media owners are only too ready to accept bookings from anyone who has the money to place them. It is interesting to observe that along with the revolution in advertising there has also been a revolution in the composition of British media; regrettable though it may appear, the viability of a newspaper or a magazine is to an almost total extent dependent on its ability to attract advertisers (the extent varies, of course, with the style of the publication, but in general the point is true), and in the context of modern news media, highly competitive and delicately costed, it is the large company with a persuasive budget which represents the target for every Fleet Street advertisement manager or representative. Whether the booking comes direct or through an advertising agency is irrelevant; revenue is revenue, no matter what rules apply in this particular game.

Indeed, many companies maintain a media evaluation department, fully equipped with all the latest quantitative techniques, merely to check the effectiveness of their agency's media skill. No agency, no matter how large (in fact, the larger the agency, the greater the danger, since its clients are likely to be more sophisticated than most), can afford to ignore this phenomenon, because it is a force which is being brought to bear directly on the agency's own lifeline, its traditional and special relationship with the organisations which have supplied its profits for so long. If the agency's media expertise is shown to be faulty (and few agencies can claim to be beyond reproach in this respect), there is a great danger that either the account will move elsewhere or that the client will assume such a psychological advantage as to make handling the account an impossibility.

Fortunately for the agencies, there are as yet few clients (as a proportion of all business organisations) who have developed this expertise to its full refinement, but the writing is on the wall. Having talked to many large companies, I am convinced that in the near future it will be the exception rather than the rule for an organisation of any magnitude not to employ a nucleus of people responsible directly to its marketing group for precise and clinical appraisals of media problems. What is more, these people will in general be better trained and fundamentally more able than most of the comparative amateurs in agency media departments; they will be mathematicians, statisticians and the like, capable of employing not only more sophisticated and advanced techniques in the solution of their problems but also a deeper and broader innate intelligence to boot.

The first effects of this development are already being felt. Some of the larger companies who have media departments of their own, and who use them to supervise the buying ability of their advertising agencies, are putting them to good effect by arranging central buying facilities whereby each of their divisions, however small their budgets, and irrespective of their agencies, can take advantage of the quantity discounts obtained in this way. One of the company's agencies will act as co-ordinator for the total purchase of space and air-time for all the company's accounts, and will be responsible for allocating it to the other agencies. This cannot be regarded as anything but the thin end of the wedge.

If this trend continues, there are likely to be shock waves throughout the advertising world. Imagine the state of the industry if both our main predictions come about: bereft of its value as a supplier of creative imagination, and shorn of its privilege as a media middleman, what will it have to offer? Its entire reason for existence will disappear, and its functions will be shared amongst a variety of separate autonomous units.

The second point is that there are signs of the growth of a completely independent media service, divorced both from the agencies and from manufacturers. Not very long ago, following their success in the United States, a number of organisations called media brokers sprang up, which, as their name suggests, were companies which buy time or space from television companies and newspapers and try to sell it to advertisers. They have not as yet been very successful, for various reasons, but the principle they represent is a significant one. One advertising agency group, KMPH, has already separated its media department from the rest of the agency, and it operates as an autonomous unit working for all the agencies in the group who pay a fee for its services. The time has not yet arrived when it will book space for companies who are not KMPH clients, but it cannot be far away. It may appear unusual for an agency to take such a revolutionary step, but it is really a defensive measure designed to protect the agency against the possibility of similar moves by independent operators, and the removal of media responsibility from the agencies.

Exactly how the responsibility will be divided between media buying services and manufacturers with their own media groups it is not easy to predict, but it is clear that it will be in these two areas that the future media function will rest. The result of a development in either direction will be an inevitable diminution of the agency's role as a planner and buyer of advertising space and air-time.

It may be asked, with some justification, why the agencies' position of media responsibility is being undermined in this way. There are two main reasons, the first of which is the theme of this book, namely that client companies are developing faster and reconciling themselves better to the business climate than the advertising agencies. Advances in other areas of business expertise have shown up the limitations of agency skills, and, impatient to bring this activity up to a standard comparable with that of the rest of their operations, clients have begun to do the job themselves; in the process, they have discovered that it is not so difficult after all.

Secondly, there has been a noticeable shift in the attitudes of the media owners, as we have seen. They have for far too long, they feel, been at the mercy of the agencies; their own rules, whereby only an accredited advertising 'agent' may qualify for a commission on bookings, have by definition given the agencies the unquestioned power and authority to determine the deployment of the nation's advertising money, and as a result the argument for the use of a particular newspaper, magazine or television area has been presented second-hand to the clients who spend that money. These rules are now being stretched almost to breaking point; it is common practice these days for a newspaper advertisement manager to visit clients direct and to negotiate the sale of space over the heads of the agency's media planners. The media owners have at last begun to appreciate the value of personal negotiation and to recognise the inhibitions of their traditional strictures on the granting of commissions. Deals such as this, while agreed bilaterally between media and client, still tend to be booked through the client's agency, but how long this strange situation will continue is a matter for conjecture.

How, then, do all these changes and developments leave the agency – or, to be more precise, how do they leave the advertising industry? We have postulated a situation in which virtually every function save that of creating advertisements will eventually be removed from the organised complex we know as the advertising agency. We might therefore be justified in saying that we have effectively pronounced a sentence of death on the agency itself and replaced it with a series of specialist units, each performing its own particular task in the advertising operation. The creative function, while notionally remaining as the sole *raison d'être* of the traditional agency, can in any case be performed better, more effectively and almost certainly more cheaply by the new consultancies or 'ideas centres' we have described; it is therefore questionable whether the agency, after the full effects of the revolution have been felt, will continue to exist at all.

These 'ideas centres' seem to me to answer far more specifically the needs of advertisers than the cumbersome, unwieldy and inappropriate machinery of today's agencies. They exist to supply the satisfaction of a need – the need for a central and fundamental theme for a company's promotion of itself and its products – rather than to complicate and obfuscate the communicational problems of industry by offering services which are neither welcome nor necessary, or by duplicating (sometimes amateurishly) the activities of a client's own marketing organisation.

Industry is looking for creative 'ideas' more than anything else. It is not even necessarily looking for the means of implementing them. One spark of original thinking is worth more than the total structure of organised advertising or all the contrived and repetitious jargon served up so predictably on the agency production line. The new centres are bringing to the business a freshness and a relevance which are good precisely because they stem from a concentration on a single task, the task of solving creative problems without the need for justification in other areas.

This gradual disintegration of the formal structure of advertising will, of course, leave behind some vestiges of its present shape. There will perhaps always be a few 'agencies' in the traditional sense who will continue to provide a 'total' advertising service based on both the creative and media functions. Such organisations may well be attractive only to small clients who either lack the resources to control their own promotional strategy or know no better; certainly, all the evidence suggests that it is from the larger agencies that the new movement is coming, since it is in these that the best talent resides, and it is the best talent which is realising the opportunities and benefits of fragmentation.

It is perhaps worth a reminder, in this context, that in any case there is within advertising today an unwritten set of rules for survival. The choice facing most smaller agencies is both simple and unpalatable: expand or expire. As in all other industries, the power and the influence are becoming concentrated into the hands of fewer and larger units. When these go, to be replaced by the specialist units we have discussed, the small agencies will have reached the limit of their expansion potential.

One of the interesting speculations in all this is the effect of these changes upon the IPA, since it is partly through the Institute's attitude (its protectionism and its faith in the commission system in particular) that the situation has developed to the point where change is desirable. Clearly, if there are no longer agencies as we know them, the IPA's terms of reference will no longer be the same. Also, if industry itself, as we have suggested, takes over most of the functions of today's agencies, there will be little except the 'hot shops' for the IPA to protect, and it is questionable whether those adventurous creative rebels would require or even tolerate such protection. It would, I suspect, represent too much of a constraint in their competitive environment to have the regulations of the Institute round their necks.

The IPA exists only because today's advertising industry exists. That industry, as we have shown, is not only sterile in the extreme; it is also constantly changing in itself to such an extent that its very personality has become at the same time both unstable and impermanent. It is becoming something new, another species, removed from its previous existence, catering for different demands and justifying itself in a different way. The conditions of life which produced the need for the maternal embrace of the Institute are, like the red flag which was once held aloft in front of the early motors, no longer applicable.

The nub of the affair must surely be that advertising will in the future belong not to the advertising agency but to a new breed of organisations. The difficulty in contemplating such a situation is that most people – advertisers and agents alike – cannot without extreme effort conceive of an arrangement different from that of today. How else, it may be asked, can advertising possibly be organised? How else can the needs of industry be satisfied? How can anyone, accustomed as he is to today's conditions, adjust his attitudes to a totally new conception of business life? This is the major gulf which must mentally be crossed; this is the Rubicon between self-deception and reality.

This, in short, is the dilemma facing the IPA. It tries, I think, albeit slowly, to adjust itself to the changing scene; but it starts from the entrenched position of believing that the future will be only a modification of the present, and not a total departure from it. It can imagine no other basis than that upon which the industry is presently founded, and consequently sees dimly, if at all, the direction the business must inevitably take. Thus, it has so irrevocably identified itself with and committed itself to the present structure – indeed, it is *part* of that structure – that any crumbling of that structure represents a crumbling of the Institute. Every new divergence from traditional methods, processes or behaviour is a further erosion of the authority vested in the IPA.

The IPA is not a separate entity. It is made up from the industry itself; its officers are active agency men. One of the arguments frequently advanced to persuade young agency people to take the Institute's examinations is that new blood is needed to populate the many committees and working parties which deal with its affairs; this supposedly adds kudos to the agencies which supply these new names, and ensures that the circular process of the industry's self-perpetuation continues. But it cannot continue for ever; for if the source of supply dries up, as it must surely do in time as more and more people leave the agencies for less traditional organisations, the IPA will become gradually more emasculated, and its effectiveness less real. It will come to depend to an ever-increasing extent for its resources on the older, less forward-looking elements of the business because the best brains will have gone elsewhere.

At what point in the process of dissolution the IPA will confess that it no longer represents the interests of the industry as a whole depends on the speed at which the changes we have described take place. Presumably, it will happen when the voices from outside the frontiers of traditionalism become stronger than those from within. At the moment, of course, we are nowhere approaching such a stage, but the process is constantly accelerating.

The IPA itself, naturally enough, finds the prospect of such a dramatic upheaval inconceivable. Members of the Institute, when asked about the future of the industry, see little of significance in the happenings of recent years. Advertising, to them, is a total concept, inextricably bound to the bodily shape of the agency; and because the agency has existed more or less in its present shape for a hundred years or so, they view it as being cloaked in immortality. Only one prominent member of the advertising Establishment (who shall for obvious reasons be nameless, but who will no doubt remember the prognostications he made in conversation with me some three or four years ago) has ever admitted that the future of advertising is anything other than the future of the agency.

Consumerism

This chapter on the changes taking place in advertising would not be complete without reference to what is surely one of the most significant symptoms of the seventies – the great wave of public concern over its own protection.

We have for many years now experienced a number of manifestations of this movement, not all of them concerned with advertised products or services; the most recent is the Longford Report on pornography. Whether such attitudes stem from a protest against the increase in so-called 'permissiveness', or from a levelling of social strata, or merely from the growing power and complexity of modern communications, it is not easy to say; but there must surely be some link, however tenuous, between the motivations prompting people to complain of moral turpitude, television programmes and the more practical considerations of commercial malpractice, shoddy products or untruthful advertising.

From the early days (in the fifties) of the Consumers' Association and the Consumer Council, we have progressed a long way. The Government is now finding it impossible to stand aside from the scene and is actively pursuing a policy of legal involvement; the Trade Descriptions Act was only the first step in this direction. In the United States, where most movements seem larger than life, Ralph Nader has apparently founded a new industry in consumer protection, and has scored some notable triumphs, particularly in the motor industry; and the American Government has reacted by introducing measures by which advertisers who have been proved to have made misleading claims can be forced to advertise a correction. A (by now) celebrated instance of this is the case of the bread manufacturer forced to buy television air-time to state publicly that his claim of fewer calories per slice was based on the fact that his bread was sliced more thinly than his competitors'.

The attitude of the advertising industry in Britain to these pressures from the public and the Government shows an interesting historical development. In the early days, it tended to ignore them or at best damn them with faint praise. The membership of the consumer protection organisations, it claimed, was too small to be significant, and in any case there was so little irresponsible advertising that it was hardly worth making a fuss about.

Now the interesting thing is that while membership of those organisations is still small (compared with the total consumer population it is minimal) the attitudes they represent are far more widespread. Furthermore, as a result of a recent survey it was discovered by a rather surprised advertising industry that the majority of people regarded British advertising as bad, dull and irrelevant.

This revelation has led to a remarkable series of advertisements by the Advertising Association to the effect that 'advertising's first duty is to the consumer', a claim which I cannot remember having heard before in all my years in the business. It is a piece of self-delusion worthy of Quixote himself.

Clearly, what has happened is that the industry has (correctly) identified the cause, and has come to the conclusion that the best way to beat the protectionists is to join them. The result is that the volte-face has been so sudden and so dramatic that it is totally unbelievable; time was when advertising justified itself in terms of its duty to its clients or to industry in general, looking upon itself as a professional (i.e. competent) extension of its clients' activity, dedicated like its clients to the profit motive. The only consumers to whom it could be said to have had a first duty were its shareholders.

Now, apparently, advertising can run with the hare and hunt with the hounds. Its argument is that it is acting as a sort of catalyst on the ethical aspects of its clients' behaviour. While we exist, claim the agencies, to serve our clients and sell their products, we shall always put the consumer first; not for us the sordid considerations of profit from the sale of a product which satisfies a need; not for us the maximisation of benefit from selling to consumers what they never knew they wanted until we told them; not for us the concentration on the principles of business management; rather, we must uphold the welfare of the people and the sanctity of common rights.

This is all very strange, and clearly unacceptable. It represents a fundamental error of judgement on the part of the industry, for it disobeys a cardinal rule of advertising practice, which is that much more can be gained by turning public attitudes to advantage than by trying to change them. If public opinion of British advertising is low, the answer lies not in trying to alter that opinion but in improving the object of it. It is arrogance to conclude that because people don't like your product there must be something wrong with them. It is also an insult to their intelligence.

Instead of attempting to bring about the impossible by creating an immediate metamorphosis of attitudes which have been built up and consolidated over many years, the industry would have done far better to have been honest. Its earlier (and often voiced) argument was not only true but also far more believable: irresponsible and untruthful advertising *is* comparatively rare, and while many of our current advertisements may be technically or aesthetically poor they are not for these reasons ethically reprehensible. Furthermore – and this is the important point – if companies were not in business to make profits they would have no need to sell, and if there were no need to sell there would be no advertising; the industry is deluding everybody, including itself, if it tries to establish any other order of priorities. Of course it is part of advertising's duty to be honest, but this is not because it is particularly conscious of its moral obligations; it is because it knows only too well from years of experience that it can only fool people once, and that it is the second – the repeat – purchase which confirms a campaign's effectiveness. There is an old saying that if there is anything worse than bad advertising for a good product it is good advertising for a bad one. People are not going to rush back to buy something a second time if the first time they bought it was the result of a misconception of its nature or if it failed to live up to the claims made for it by its advertising.

Thus, if advertising has an obligation to tell the truth, that obligation is to its clients and not to the consumer, because the consequences to its clients if the obligation is not honoured can be disastrous. Consumerism may well have made advertising more alert to the need for truth, as indeed have the many official controls to which the business is subjected, but in the final analysis it is the client whose interests are best served by honesty.

It may be asked, in view of the growth of consumer protection movements, whether it is altogether a good thing for advertising to be breaking away from its traditional structures and reforming into a less integrated and looser operation over which the Institute and the Association have virtually no jurisdiction. Does this weaken its strength in the face of criticism? This can be answered only by another question: what evidence is there that advertising, as most of it is organised today, has succeeded either in creating for itself a respectable reputation or in answering criticisms levelled against it? From our analysis, it would seem that in any case industry will itself take over much of the responsibility for its own advertising, which may well result in a more balanced and coherent apologia; for the rest – the creative function in the hands of the ideas centres and consultancies – who knows but that it will set up its own committee to speak on its behalf?

If this should happen, it is most earnestly to be hoped that the new body will begin by defining accurately what the terms of reference of the business are, and continue by speaking out at every opportunity to defend it in language which does not, like the Advertising Association's recent campaign, demand an intolerable suspension of disbelief. Only in this way will public attitudes towards advertising begin to improve. As things are at the moment, the argument is very one-sided, and it is thus hardly surprising that consumer opinion is so markedly unfavourable and concomitant editorial comment so unsympathetic.

What the advertising industry, in the face of strong consumerist pressures, apparently fails to realise is that those very pressures are good for advertising. There are in any event so many controls on the standards of advertising that an extra one from consumers themselves should not be such a heavy cross to bear. Indeed, it can be argued that advertising should welcome this free market feedback. So much is written and spoken about the indispensability of marketing information that it is surprising that the voice of consumer protection should be so unacceptable. Few stages in the marketing process can be satisfactorily accomplished without information from the market place: a new product concept needs to be validated through concept testing; when that concept becomes a physical prototype it requires further testing through product research to remove snags and perfect its performance; the pricing policy adopted by the manufacturer cannot be established without some reference to the price the public is prepared to pay; the product's packaging needs consumer approval; and as for the product's advertising, any reputable agency will require considerable data about consumer behaviour – buying habits, frequency of purchase, motivation to buy, reference groups, usage, readership and viewership profiles, penetration studies, consumer panels, retail audits, and so on. Every piece of information about the market or the consumer, if properly used, is another insurance against failure, a greater limitation of risk.

Surely, therefore, consumer opinion as expressed through the protection groups, spontaneously and at no cost, should be regarded as further useful evidence on which to base the control of the total marketing effort, and not as a tiresome irritant? Much can be gained by co-operation between the two sides, for the alternative – fruitless disagreement – can only exacerbate the public suspicion which already exists.

Conclusion

This chapter has described some of the more significant changes which are taking place within the advertising industry, and has considered also the implications of a particularly important external factor, consumerism. In both, there is evidence to suggest that the main body of opinion amongst advertising people is weighted against change, either of attitude or structure, and that this complacency is doing harm to advertising. Even advertising's own trade journals (and, to some extent, the national press also), while being conscious of what is happening, seem strangely unable to recognise the implications of it.

The chapter which follows examines some of these implications, and the final chapter tries to show what the British advertising industry will look like in twenty years' time, how it will operate and what relationships it will have with its clients.

Chapter 7

Advertising Man

In the first chapter of this book we traced the development of advertising through the ages. One of the periods we reviewed we called the golden age, the age of Leverhulme, Barratt, Carroll, Benson and the rest, during the years at the end of the last century and the beginning of this.

If we were to analyse the secret of the greatness of these men, the reason why they were so successful in their use of advertising, we should find two main attributes above the rest: firstly, they were essentially creative people, who were able to touch the central nerve of communication and whose imagination was boundless; secondly, they were men of enormously broad vision, who saw in advertising not an isolated function but an inseparable part of their total business. They were less concerned with details and technicalities than they were with grand strategy; they could turn their hands to any aspect of commercial life and be more successful than other men; they were generalists *par excellence.*

The same is true of most of the giants of later advertising. Few men who have ever achieved fame in the business (men like Crawford, Ogilvy, Hobson and, more recently, Bernstein) have been far away from the creative function. Even those whose main operational role has been in another area – media, research, account management – have been able to appreciate, contribute to and clarify creative affairs. They have identified themselves with the focal point of advertising while at the same time having the breadth of outlook indispensable to the acceptance of advertising as a total operation and not merely the sum of its parts. These, too, in their way could be called generalists rather than specialists in any particular function.

The purpose of this chapter is to suggest that the changes which were discussed in Chapter 6 are gradually producing a new breed of advertising people who have more in common with the generalists of early advertising than with the narrow functional specialists who populate most of the advertising agencies of today. The wheel has turned full circle.

When advertising first became a major force in the exchange of goods between manufacturer and customer as a result of wider horizons created by the mass production and new distributive facilities of the industrial revolution, it was stimulated, and to a large extent implemented, by the men who made the products. It was the manufacturer who decided what he would say, how he would say it, where and when; the agencies, such as they were, he tended to regard merely as the tools of his trade. Because of this, there was a *completeness* about his business operations which did not reappear to anything like the same extent until the corporate identity exercises of recent years; of course, his attitude was based on intuitive business sense rather than on any formalised philosophy, though the formalisation itself clearly represents a conceptualised set of experiences. A typical example of a modern diagrammatical illustration of the interrelationship between the four dimensions of design for corporate purposes is shown in Fig. 7; our old manufacturer would be puzzled by this, largely because of the unfamiliarity of the terms used, but he would nevertheless in all probability have put the concept into practice.

As a result of the way in which advertising (and the communications business as a whole) has developed, it is given to few industrialists these days to exercise the same degree of influence over their own advertising. There are some (what advertising man has not met at least one?) who still, it is true, insist on personal responsibility for their promotional programme, but this responsibility is passive rather than active since the onus of creativity is squarely on the agency's head. There is a gap between the manufacturer's personal involvement with his business and the involvement of the agency; this is inevitable in the complex environment of today, but it is not helped by the additional functional fragmentation of the agency itself. One needs only to examine the advertisements in any issue of a morning newspaper, women's magazine or trade journal to realise how far they depart in character and identity from the business they aim to promote: this tends to produce in the reader's mind what teachers of business management (always ready to cloak fairly simple and straightforward concepts in a web of unintelligibility) have

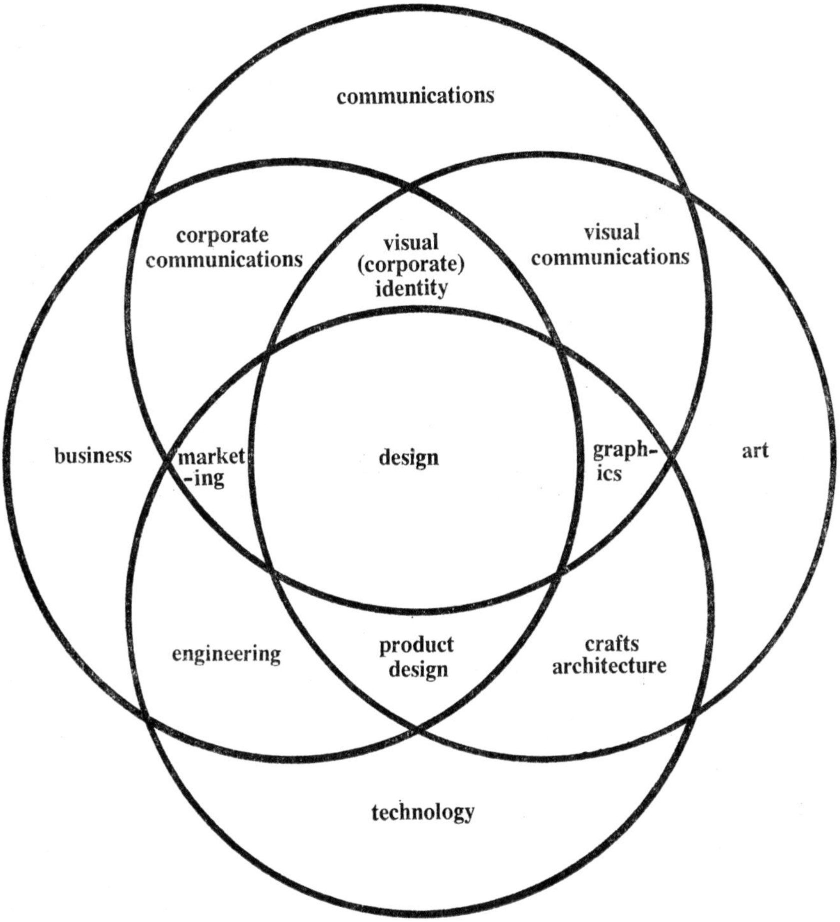

Fig. 7 The four dimensions of design and their interrelationship for corporate purposes

(Reproduced with the kind permission of Dr R. H. Beck from the Council of Industrial Design's booklet *A Management Guide to Corporate Identity*, 1971)

called 'cognitive dissonance', which being translated means the incompatibility of perceived evidence. Outrageous though some of the early advertisements were, they at least had the flavour of the advertiser in them.

Now, what is interesting about the growing trend to creative consultancies and the fragmentation of advertising functions is that this new kind of creative service entails a much more complete involvement with clients' operations. Divorced as they are from the many ancillary services of the normal agency, the consultants, by concentrating single-mindedly on the creative problem, are beginning to discover how broad that problem really is. Whereas in the agency they had left matters of research and media to their respective specialist departments, they now frequently find that they themselves are not only interested in such matters, because they impinge upon their own area, but are also, to a very large extent, competent to discuss them intelligently and with purpose. They are thus, paradoxically, through increasing their specialism also becoming more generalistic in their approach.

Furthermore, because their involvement is so complete (as a result of their work on such projects as corporate identity programmes), they have realised that the relationship which exists between their clients and themselves is far closer and more productive than that which they experienced in the agency. In this respect, while the consultant clearly has his living to earn, he is much less of a 'company man' than his agency counterpart. We saw in Chapter 2 how frequently the loyalties of agency men can become confused; in the consultancy the opportunities for such confusion are rare, precisely because of the basis of their client relationship.

It is perhaps worth digressing for a moment to indicate how fortunate the independent consultant is in this respect. Advertising is still very much an unquantifiable process. Thus, the formal structure of the traditional agency tends to impose unnatural constraints on individual opinions as a result of the inevitable hierarchy of authority and responsibility. Few advertising campaigns are devised without some differences of personal attitudes, either between account manager and creative group or between account management and agency management. Not only this; there are also frequent conflicts of opinion as to how particular accounts should be handled, a situation which is bound to arise sooner or later when line management responsibility is vested in the hands of people who see clients relatively infrequently and operational responsibility in the hands of people who see clients almost every day. Half of the column inches of the communications trade journals are taken up every week with stories of such disagreements; agencies have been known to break up as a result, and accounts to change hands. Such problems are not part of the consultant's life.

In Chapters 4 and 5 it was shown that creative people are, and always have been, different in attitude and temperament from other people in advertising, and that this is the major justification for their remaining independent from the rest of industry in the new advertising set-up. They are the strong element of the communications industry; they have always been something special. At the same time they have represented perhaps the broadest thinking in the business: their peculiar ability not to be 'confused by the facts' has enabled them to take a *total* view of advertising affairs, uncomplicated by the nuances of research data or executive attitudes; they have traditionally consistently refused to be diverted from the central issue of producing a good advertisement. In this sense they possess a far more general attitude than the rest of their agency colleagues; they are capable of seeing what advertising is really all about without having to persuade themselves (like media men or account managers) that they are indispensable. There is no need for this: they *are* indispensable.

On the other hand, the other specialists in agencies are very vulnerable. It could be argued, I suppose, that account executives, because of the peculiar nature of their job, need to be especially capable of performing it; but this is true of almost any function, since it is evident that some people perform particular tasks better than others. It is certainly true of the media function, which is compounded of a mixture of experience and technical knowledge. Any intelligent person, given the opportunity to learn the tricks of the trade, could perform the tasks required of all agency specialists except those concerned with creative affairs. In Chapter 3 we discussed the recruitment and training of advertising people, and we showed that it was difficult to recruit good account executives; but this was because the people who would best perform the tasks of an account executive would also, far more rewardingly, perform the function of a marketing executive in industry. The problem is therefore one not of discovery but of attraction.

The point is that, in all functions save the creative one, training and the ability to assimilate experience are on a par with intelligence; they are functions to be learnt, not functions which require a certain attitude of mind. This means that industry is not going to find it difficult (indeed, it is not finding it difficult) to assume the responsibility for these functions itself.

Thus the creative consultancies are both a step forward towards a more logical form of advertising service and a strange echo of what advertising used to be. The men who populate them in ever-increasing numbers are in no doubt as to what they are there to do, and what can be left to the client (in contrast to the agencies who are in great confusion on this point). They do not need to justify themselves on any grounds other than their own creative competence.

It is likely that the advertising agencies of the early years of the century would quickly recognise the type of person now working in freelance consultancy. The difference, of course, is that the old-timers would still need to draw their income from their clients' media expenditure, but they would sympathise with the desire of their modern counterpart to be centrally involved; they would, I am sure, find the departmentalisation and specialisation of the modern agency repugnant.

Another important implication of the consultancy development is that at last there will exist the opportunity for all aspects of the design function to be centralised under one roof. In the past, advertising agencies have concerned themselves with little other than the advertising campaign itself; true, they have occasionally been asked to produce a new pack design or a special label, and they have from time to time been involved in point-of-sale material, but here their terms of reference have ended. They have rarely been consulted on, for example, the design of an exhibition stand or the livery of a client's transport fleet, or his letterheads, invoices and compliments slips. These are all part of the overall function of design, as illustrated in Fig. 7, which for industry culminates in the conception of a corporate identity.

The new breed of creative consultants, no longer dependent on media expenditure for their income, can consequently adopt a total attitude to design. They can, in all they do for their clients, pursue a consistent policy of presenting the same corporate image. Their terms of reference are no longer merely those of producing an advertising campaign once a year but the entire corporate communications spectrum. They will identify themselves fully with their clients' total business objectives (not only their promotional goals) and will apply themselves to the task of achieving those objectives in every aspect of the communication process. Thus, while they will still undoubtedly be concerned with the preparation of advertising material, this will be only a part of their complete task.

This wider responsibility is by no means as easy as it may sound.

The fact that companies who have never adopted a coherent attitude to their corporate image can be using as many as 40 or 50 functional types of stationery design alone, emanating from about 180 different sources,[1] indicates the problems involved in the creation of a company identity. Add to this the multiplicity of uses of company name-styles on vans, lorries, uniforms, hoardings, leaflets, advertisements and even the products themselves, and the task becomes formidable. Furthermore, when the consultant has rationalised the situation by creating the means whereby some common identity can be attached to all these things, his problem is not necessarily solved: unless the person to whom he is responsible in the client's organisation has the authority to implement the changes which are recommended, the consultant may have to face the onerous task of convincing other people of their value.

The result of a rational corporate image programme, of course, is an eventual reduction in costs. Even though the change itself may be expensive, the subsequent savings achieved through standardisation of design can be impressive. Apart from the economies of scale resulting from simplified printing requirements, sign production and other material savings, there are also hidden benefits (mostly incalculable) through improved communications, better customer relations and more favourable public attitudes, which cannot help but improve a company's trading climate.

In our examination of the implications of the changes being effected in advertising we have been concentrating on creativity. This is inevitable, since it is only the creative function that has any real right to a separate existence and any proper claim to the advertising title. To examine the advertising industry of the future will be to examine the people who create it: these will be 'advertising' people; the rest will be technicians in marketing services.

Nevertheless, it is interesting to contemplate the broader effects of the change. For example, the ripples sent out from the centre of the advertising pond are likely to upset the hitherto undisturbed waters of the media industry, in particular the old traditions of Fleet Street. In Chapter 6 it was pointed out that already some of the media owners, realising the constraints attendant on a dependence upon the agency for the sale of their space and air-time, are beginning to make direct

[1] F. H. K. Henrion, 'How Designers Serve Corporate Needs', *A Management Guide to Corporate Identity* (Council of Industrial Design, 1971).

approaches to industry, and that manufacturers, more competent than ever before to evaluate and select media for their products and services, are prepared to negotiate without their advertising agencies. It was shown that for the most part any bookings agreed to under such circumstances tended to be channelled through the agencies, in order that the commissions offered by the media may be obtained, and thus that the necessary creative work may be paid for.

On the other hand, if the commission system were to disappear (and extensive reference will be made to this possibility in the next chapter), and if creative service is supplied on a consultancy basis rather than through the traditional agency channels, what is to happen to the rules set up by the various media and advertising bodies governing the granting of commissions? Clearly it would be to the advantage of the media owners to be paid the full card rate instead of having to discount 15 per cent on every sale, but, by the same token, manufacturers will not take kindly to the prospect of having to pay both a fee to their creative consultants and the full price to the media.

There are various possible escapes from the impasse. For example, the media owners could abolish the commission system and reduce their rates accordingly; this would probably involve a differentiated scale of charges for industrial and private advertisers, and would automatically stimulate a movement towards a fee system by the IPA, since it has to work closely with the NPA, the Newspaper Society, the PPA and the ITCA. Alternatively, commission facilities could be extended beyond recognised agencies to manufacturers themselves; this is really only another way of doing the same thing, and would again encourage a movement towards fees. The third possibilitity is the least likely: newspaper and magazine owners and television contractors could abolish altogether their published rates and negotiate for individual contracts with manufacturers in a free market, creating a kind of 'floating' rate, like the arrangement which exists in some European countries; but this would be confusing, and would almost certainly operate to the disadvantage of the smaller advertiser whose lower budget would limit his negotiating power. Even with circumstances as they are now, the privileges resulting from large appropriations are significant, and it is difficult to see the media industry taking steps to make the situation worse. The final solution, of course, depends on the interpretation placed on developments in advertising by the media themselves, but it is fairly clear that present arrangements will need to be modified.

Other repercussions will be felt in the area of marketing research. With the transfer of most of the control of the promotional effort from the agency to the client, the source of income for the many research organisations who currently depend on the advertising industry for their revenue will change. According to a survey conducted by the British Institute of Management twelve years ago,[1] the ratio of research expenditure to total turnover by advertising agencies was greater than that of any other industrial group (0·82 per cent against a mean figure of 0·7 per cent and ratios of 0·04 per cent and 0·08 per cent for industrial goods manufacturers and consumer goods manufacturers respectively). While the figures shown by the survey may not necessarily be wholly accurate, since only about a third of the questionnaires was returned, they do point to an enormous difference between advertising agencies and the rest of industry. Furthermore, it is generally accepted that in unit terms (that is, the number of individual research projects commissioned) agencies have in the past been responsible for a greater number than any other type of business organisation.

The BIM survey is now clearly out of date and a more recent study may well show a different picture. What is certain is that along with the manufacturer's increasing responsibility for his own advertising strategy will come a decrease in the amount of research commissioned by his agency. Admittedly, this will not be a real change in financial terms, since much of the research organised by agencies is paid for by clients anyway, but it will represent a significant shift of responsibility and should cause the research companies to alter the focus of their own selling efforts. This will be true of all types of research, from concept and product testing to communications research, motivational studies and the like. These are likely to become more and more the responsibility of manufacturers themselves.

It is in fact surprising that advertising agencies have continued for so long to instigate so much marketing research. After all, the days when advertising was a move ahead of the rest of industry in marketing techniques (of which research is one of the most significant) have passed; if anything, advertising agencies are now some considerable way behind

[1] *Survey of Marketing Research in Great Britain* (BIM Information summary, 1962), No. 97.

their clients in this respect. Perhaps the answer may be found in the fact that, although the agencies have been the principals in their research projects, the instigation of the desire for research has been largely in the hands of their clients. It is impossible to calculate the precise demand for research originating from the agencies themselves.

One of the services provided by the agencies, about which little has been said in an examination of the changing face of the industry, is that of production (both of print and television material) and of print itself. The people who staff these departments rarely originate in advertising. In the case of television, they come either from film production companies or from the less well-defined area of script writing. As for press production and printing, staff are drawn from typesetters and blockmakers, or from printers themselves. How are these going to be affected by the changes?

It stands to reason that if the creative function, which is the provider of material for production, moves away from the agency, there will be no work for production departments. Where, then, will they go? There are two possibilities, both for television and print, and each needs to be considered in turn.

In the case of television production, there is an extremely close relationship between it and the creative function itself; this relationship is far closer than that between the creation and production of print material, for the simple reason that the creative process is still continuing during the production of a film. While the script-writer may create a particular concept or storyline, there remains much for the director and producer to add: specific effects may be suggested either before or during filming which will help to communicate more strongly what the script-writer has written, and these will be welcomed by the script-writer as part of the film's creation. In this sense, a film idea can never be finally evaluated until the film itself has been shot, printed, and edited.

Because of this close relationship, it is very necessary for film writers and film producers to maintain maximum contact; they can never operate very far from each other. It is likely, therefore, that one of two things will happen: either the new consultancies will retain on their own staff people who will be competent to produce film material (in conjunction with the film production companies), or working arrangements will be established with freelance film producers for this purpose. There are, of course, many television and film writers who are competent producers in their own right; these will naturally find a happy hunting ground in the consultancies.

Press production and print is a different case. Here the function is a purely mechanical one, with few if any opportunities for creativity. Press and print material depends for most of its quality on its original design and the artwork from which it is produced. There is thus a far less intimate relationship with creative people (the art directors who provide the work). The two possible developments in this area are perhaps less easy to evaluate since it is questionable to what degree manufacturers will be prepared to involve themselves in this particular function. However, it seems fairly certain that, since the consultancies will continue to have a substantial demand for production services, they will need to deal either direct with suppliers or through some kind of middleman; in either event they will require someone on their staff with the requisite technical knowledge. This will be particularly true of print work. As for the production of press advertisements, where the procedure has usually involved the delivery of the material to the newspapers themselves, it is unlikely that the consultancies, being removed from the media operation, will wish to provide such a service. The logical location of the function is with the manufacturer himself, since, as has been indicated, it is quite clearly separate from the creative operation.

It can be seen that the fragmentation of the agency is producing a new alignment of advertising services; some will be retained by the consultancies, some will become completely independent, and the rest will be taken over by the manufacturers. More will be said about this in the next chapter, but it is interesting to see how the structures of a hundred-odd years need to be bent and remoulded to suit the changed business climate.

We have discussed at some length the implications of the changes affecting the advertising industry from the point of view of advertising itself. We cannot complete our discussion without some examination of the effects these changes may have on the people to whom the bulk of advertising is directed, the British public.

It could be argued that advertising, in divorcing itself from the realities of business life, has by the same token lost touch with its customers, the consumers and industrial buyers on which it depends for its existence.

Whether this is in fact what has happened we can only guess: as has been said before, the evaluation of an advertising campaign is something that can be done only with a full knowledge of the problem it sets out to solve. Nevertheless, there is some justification for believing that the business has become so inward-looking that its language has assumed an identity of its own quite removed from the language used by its audience.

If this is so, the communication process is being jammed by less than adequate comprehension on the part of the receiver. The freshness of attitude brought into play by the new consultancies should go a long way towards overcoming this problem and establishing once more an effective link between advertiser and audience. It is one of the hoped-for results of the more catholic approach adopted by these new types of advertising men that their communications should increase both in power and relevance; and this, after all, is what the business should be striving for.

The natural effect of this should be that the unfavourable public attitude which was discussed in the previous chapter will begin to moderate. Much of the antagonism which exists today towards advertising stems from precisely that jamming of the communication process referred to above; and with improved reception should come increased sympathy and involvement. Thus, the new communicators, while not deliberately embarking upon a public relations programme for the industry, will, by doing the best job for their clients, be creating the best possible image for themselves Which just goes to show the importance of doing things right.

Chapter 8

Advertising Tomorrow

Introduction

What, then, of the future? How are the upheavals, the undercurrents of change and the new patterns of industry going to affect advertising over the next five, ten or twenty years? Have we enough evidence now to say with any certainty how our business organisations, the fount from which all advertising budgets flow, will spend their money?

It would be rash for anyone to be too dogmatic. As we have seen, advertising has reached the watershed of its development, and many things can happen during the next few years to change the picture, even change the trends which are now beginning to emerge; advertising (that is, advertising people) is a fickle lady, and could well in the manner of her kind decide either to follow fashion or protest against it. The question is, can she afford to linger over the choice?

We need to look back over the chapters of this book before we can set about formulating our prognosis, because it is only through encapsulating the argument contained in them that conclusions can be drawn. Those conclusions will necessarily be handmaidens to events: if the future proves them wrong, so be it. Yet unless the advertising industry is prepared to examine its prospects, unless it is ready to recognise the forces which may shape its future, and unless it decides how to equip itself to meet new pressures, new constraints and new opportunities, it will fail; the weak will weaken and the strong will not grow stronger. Like man himself, advertising has reached the point of having the power to control its own destiny; and, like man, it could destroy itself.

This analogy of human evolution can be carried further, in that the probability of self-annihilation is small. Just as man has already seen the dire results of his own power and has thus been taught a salutary lesson, so can advertising now survey the forces at work within itself and learn to its own advantage how best to treat them. It will be the able, the intelligent and the perspicacious advertising people who will accept and follow the dynamics of change, and they will succeed; the feeble, timid and reactionary will protest, resist and disappear.

Before we go on to summarise our argument, there is one final point to be made. The evidence we have examined suggests that the British advertising industry, for so long influenced and stimulated by American example, is at last beginning to evolve as an entity in its own right. How far this phenomenon is the result of conditions peculiar to the British industrial economy is hard to say, but it is surely beyond coincidence that its emergent symptoms have manifested themselves only in the last few years, a period notable for exceptional financial stresses and constraints never previously experienced by this traditionally successful business.

It has always been a fact of British advertising life that most of our biggest and most powerful agencies are American owned: the biggest of them all – J. Walter Thompson – is the prime example. There have been few truly big British agencies, and most of these have now stretched their hands across the herring pond – Hobson Bates, the London Press Exchange, Mather and Crowther – with the result that until comparatively recently it was reasonably safe to predict that what happened in America would happen in Britain after an interval of around three years (and, incidentally, that it would happen in the rest of Europe about three years after that).

This influence has been largely a matter of the development of techniques, and, now that these techniques have reached the stage where further improvement is only marginal, advertising on both sides of the Atlantic has evolved to a point from which it can go no further along the same line: it must either change its entire structure and become, if not something different, something with a different relationship to the rest of industry, or it must merely enmesh itself in an increasingly complicated and intricate web of its own making.

British advertising, in short, has learned all it can from its mentor and guide. It has begun to notice that what suits America does not necessarily suit the UK. What is more, it has begun to acknowledge its own environment.

This is not to say that future developments in Britain will differ significantly from those in the USA – only that they will happen largely free from American influence. It is well to recognise this, since we shall be witnessing for the first time an independent movement in British advertising, stimulated entirely by events in Britain.

Recapitulation

The analysis of British advertising contained in the earlier chapters has traced the growth of advertising up to the complex modern agency; it has shown how it functions and how it serves its clients; it has examined the way in which the advertising business has gradually become aware of the power it wields and the extent to which it attempts to protect itself against public suspicion and opprobrium through an almost ostrich-like desire to hide away its head in the sand of pseudo-professionalism.

Further, we have seen some of the anomalies inherent in its behaviour: the commission system, where remuneration depends less on the work done than the money spent by the client; the marketing/creative dilemma, involving much duplication of effort between client and agency and highlighting many inadequacies on the agency's part, particularly in the area of new product development; the agency's failure to realise its single really strong point, the creative expertise which clients so studiously avoid; and what we have called the 'new business business', where even the agencies themselves openly flaunt the very rules with which they have agreed to protect themselves.

Our investigation next surveyed the inbred nature of the business, with its inexorable drift towards greater and greater specialisation in different functional areas; how advertising sometimes appears to exist purely for its own gratification, with its awards and prizes granted on no other criterion than subjective opinion; and how these attitudes, divorced as they are from a consciousness of any central scheme mutually beneficial to both agencies and their clients, militate against the chances of effective and relevant business planning.

The need for new thinking and new structures has been stressed, although their nature and shape were not specified; and a word of warning was sounded in case this need was ignored. We examined the specific requirements of the agency's clients and found that they were as often as not precisely what the agency is best able, yet so frequently fails, to provide – high quality creative thinking and quick and efficient service.

We have seen how some of the traditional agency structures are beginning to crumble, being replaced by independent specialists who have accepted *de facto* a situation which already exists *de jure*; and how the major problem facing the smaller agency can be resolved in only two ways, expansion or extinction.

Finally, the last chapter indicated the way in which this disintegration of the agency's cellular structure represents an ironic return to the all-round advertising talents of the early days; 'advertising man' is once more beginning to emerge from his long sleep.

The Future

There can be little doubt that this trend will continue and accelerate, and that advertising in the future will need to tailor itself to industry's needs more appropriately than it does now.

In Chapter 2 we examined advertising in the context of social and economic life. We saw how it justified itself by raising living standards and stimulating demand for the products and services offered by industry. Whatever its faults (and there are many abuses in its practice), it will always be a part – a very necessary part – of our lives. No successful commercial venture can properly exist without it, and not one of us can honestly say that he has not at times derived some benefit from it.

The question is therefore not one of whether but rather of how advertising will operate in the future. The answer depends on two considerations: firstly, what do clients seek, and secondly, what do they regard as a fair price to pay for it? We shall discuss these in turn.

It is a curious fact that, under the present agency system, clients by and large pay no more for good work than bad. The commission arrangement is a great leveller: clients move their accounts for all kinds of reasons, but rarely, if ever, for reasons of costs. It would be difficult to find any other purchase made by industry which is made without question of price. Plant and machinery, transport and distribution services, raw materials, office equipment, heating and catering systems, even staff, are all carefully costed, and their value calculated by balancing quality against price through one sort of cost-benefit analysis or another. Why should advertising be different?

It is true that most major industrial companies still recognise some economic advantage in employing an advertising agency instead of attempting to plan and implement their own publicity effort direct with the media owners themselves. They feel that an agency not only provides these services more cheaply through the application of overheads to a wide range of accounts and clients, but also brings a higher quality of creative thinking to advertising problems through the experience gained from a great variety of different products and markets.

However, this decision on industry's part is based on an evaluation of the use of advertising agencies in general, because agencies are, by and large, the only means it has of implementing its promotional effort; it accepts unquestioningly that one agency's charges will be more or less the same as another's. The reason is not hard to find. The aura of professionalism projected by the advertising industry has deluded even its clients; they have been lulled into an unthinking acceptance of the false hypothesis on which advertising's financial systems are based, and as yet only a few have recognised the possibility of any better alternative. This has resulted in the strange situation to which reference has just been made, in which the selection of an agency is a decision removed entirely from criteria of cost.

So what is it that clients want? Many surveys, initiated mostly by the IPA or its member agencies, have been conducted to answer this question. The purpose of these surveys has inevitably always been the same: to identify precise client needs so that agencies may tailor their products to satisfy those needs – just as an agency would approach the problems of establishing accurate brand placements for its clients' products. The two requirements which consistently feature at the top of the list in the results of these surveys are, as we have seen, creative excellence and efficient service; media planning usually comes a poor third. (Incidentally, when the agencies come to devise advertising based on this information, and run campaigns promoting their own talents, the results are frequently disastrous: it is often remarked that the worst advertising an agency produces is the campaign it runs for itself – perhaps a further symptom of the introspective nature of the business).

In the light of this evidence, it seems absurd that the most competitive ingredients of an agency's appeal – its creative expertise and its standard of service – should be unquantifiable in terms of cost. If we approach a solicitor to ask him to handle the sale of a house, we can expect to pay a fixed scale of charges, laid down by the Law Society, in respect of certain legal processes, but, even so, costs will vary between solicitors for other services; and, outside the professions, we encounter significantly different prices for the same item of work. We should, for instance, receive quotations across a wide range if we asked several builders to build a house according to an agreed specification, or heating engineers to install a central heating system; the difference in the quotations offered would be explained by one of two causes: either the firms concerned would be working to different levels of profit or they would be basing their estimates on different standards of quality. In either event, we should make the decision as to which to accept on the criterion of standard of work offered compared with quoted cost. We might be prepared to accept lower standards for less cost, or we might agree to pay more for higher quality; and our attitude would be influenced both by our own experience of the quality of individual firms' work and by what the firms themselves and other people – our friends and acquaintances – say about it.

It is precisely this comparison with other services which makes the way in which advertising earns its money (and the way in which it sometimes makes money without earning it) so unrealistic in the business world of today. The fact that a slow fragmentation is taking place in the agency world, and the evidence that even some of our larger agencies are now beginning to accept the fee as a more reasonable basis of revenue than the commission system, both point to the way in which the anomaly will be resolved.

We must expect to see, I think, advertising services sold on the open market like any other product, untrammelled by contracts or binding agreements. A client will be free to approach one or more of the 'ideas centres' discussed in Chapter 6, to ask them to put a price on their services for solving his problem, and to accept or reject that price as he thinks fit. The price will refer specifically to the standard of creative service and will be divorced from the size of the client's media budget (the placing of which will be handled separately, possibly by a media planning company, on the basis of the amount of time and effort involved).

Fees will really come into their own as the standard system of charging only when the creative consultancy has largely taken the place of the existing agency structure as the natural advertising service. The reason is that there are many problems involved in establishing a satisfactory level of fees on individual accounts in agencies as they are organised today. If all media commissions are to be rebated, the agreement as to what work the fee will cover, and what it will not, will need to be very precise and unequivocal in order to avoid arguments and recriminations between agency and client; furthermore, the agreement will need to be reviewed at frequent intervals (at least annually) to allow increases or decreases in workload to be recognised. If these precautions are not observed, time may be wasted and confidence impaired during important campaigns when this can be least afforded.

This is the prime reason why agencies have remained wedded to the commission system when all logic cries out for its abolition; it is an easier, if less appropriate, method of money-making than the fee system. There is however another reason, which will also cease to apply when consultancies prevail. There can be no doubt that the increased revenue obtained by agencies through fees from clients with small media budgets will be more than cancelled out by the much larger losses of income incurred through the change from commission to fees by clients with large budgets; for, in the few cases where fees have been agreed with clients spending large amounts of money on media advertising, it is questionable whether they are as profitable as commission on turnover. The change has been made in some cases at the client's request, and in these instances the agency has little alternative but to accept if it wishes to retain the account.

This raises an important point: the agencies themselves may be aware all the time that the fee system is the more equitable, but are resisting it except in the case of small clients. If this is so, it is deplorable; it calls into question the business efficiency and honesty of the industry, and represents a tacit admission on its part that the commission arrangement is unsatisfactory in all respects save that of making more than a fair profit. In the modern commercial climate this alone is enough to imperil the future of the advertising agency, for no financial arrangement based on such a tenuous principle can survive the questioning and cost-conscious scrutiny of the new generation of industrial management.

The stimulus for change will come partly from inside and partly from outside the advertising business. On the one hand, the agencies will come to realise that their structures are no longer appropriate to the demands of industry. We have seen, for instance, the reduction in importance of agency marketing departments, from a comprehensive strategic planning unit to a mere service group providing only reheated secondary data and possessing no responsibility for recommendation, as a direct result of the development and perfection of clients' own marketing skills; we have also seen how this has forced true marketing men out of the agencies and 'across the fence' to join the clients they previously served.

Also, many other agency functions, apart from creative operations, have begun to establish their own separate industries. Market research has, of course, always been a business in its own right, but in addition there has been a rapid growth in the number of merchandising and sales promotion companies, an activity which the agencies have by and large spurned because it is largely independent of media commission; the profits earned by these companies must cause agencies considerable pain. Design groups, too, have broken away to concentrate on packaging, point-of-sale and print; and most recently we have witnessed the appearance of media brokers who perform an isolated media function. Expert media planners are thus using their talents to provide freelance media advice divorced from the formal agency structure At the moment it is not easy to see how these units will eventually overcome the difficulties of recognition by the media owners in order to qualify for buying discounts; it is certain, however, that as freelance media groups increase their buying power through greater turnover the media owners will find some means of bending the rules to accommodate them.

Once the financial viability of freelance operations had been established by creative people, this functional fragmentation was predictable. The two most significant developments outside the creative area are without doubt the proliferation of merchandising and sales promotion organisations, referred to above, and the rapid growth of marketing consultancies; it is in these two areas that there will perhaps be the fastest increase of activity, and it is worth looking at each in turn.

The agencies have only themselves to blame for the explosive developments in merchandising companies. It has been clear for a long time that competition for consumer loyalty is concentrating increasingly on the point of purchase; the growth of self-service and supermarket trading has taken away from manufacturers much of the influence they used to exercise over consumer buying habits and has transferred it to the retail organisations themselves. Thus, even before the economic depression of the late sixties which prompted manufacturers to reduce media budgets in favour of below-the-line promotional expenditure calculated to produce more immediate and more measurable effect, there was a very pronounced rise in merchandising operations. Unhappily for the agencies, they failed to capitalise on the trend, and as a result of inadequate service in this vital function they left the field wide open for the specialist organisations to spring up. These are now very big business indeed, and offer clients advice and operational control on all aspects of sales promotion, from premium offers to personality parades. Ironically, as in the case of the creative consultancies, some of their best clients are the agencies themselves.

It has been shown that most major agency clients are now totally competent to formulate, implement and control their own marketing operations. Indeed, in the majority of high-volume fast-moving packaged goods industries it is marketing management which is the driving force behind, and arbiter of, product planning. Consequently, agency marketing departments tend to be underutilised and financially depressive, except for the occasions when they are called upon to operate on behalf of small and less sophisticated clients. Unfortunately, in large agencies the client portfolio consists mostly of large clients, so that such opportunities are rarely offered. Good agency marketing men, therefore, have looked elsewhere for opportunities more appropriate to their ability, and they have either joined a manufacturing company or set up their own consultancies specialising in marketing advice for those companies who need it.

These consultancies will for a long time to come be satisfying a need in a particular type of company – the small to medium sized organisation which recognises the importance of marketing but cannot afford full-time staff of the right calibre. It is frequently the case that these companies, operating more often than not on shoestring budgets, can derive great benefits from experienced and professional marketing attitudes while they may not be able to support a permanent marketing director. A concentrated and purposeful analysis of their marketing needs, over a comparatively short period of time, may well provide the strategic guidelines of company policy for the next five or ten years, and at a very moderate cost. Such an intensive investigation can cost a company as little as £1,000, and can be amortised over several years of successful trading; to employ a full-time marketing director for five years could cost £25,000 or more – a high price for a small concern to pay. There is thus a ready market for these marketing skills.

In every respect, therefore, we shall see fragmentation of agency activity taking place, stimulated in large measure by people who themselves currently work in the agencies. However, there will also be promptings from outside the cloistered advertising business to make this change inevitable. Industry can go on for very little longer bearing on its back the cross that is the present structure of advertising. It will in time demand, and get, a better service – a service which more accurately represents what it wants. The business world is changing fast: it will soon no longer tolerate loose thinking, no longer accept inspired subjectivity, no longer abide by outmoded and irrelevant values; it will require a precise, true and appropriate order of things.

The reason is that nothing short of this will satisfy industry's economic needs. Already there are signs that the ideas of the old economists will no longer work: successive governments have provided sufficient evidence that little economic theory works in practice, and at last the results of the second industrial revolution can be seen. High unemployment is now not just evidence of industrial depression. It goes far more deeply than that: industry simply needs less labour, because it is more efficient, more automated, more quick. Furthermore, it is more conscious than ever before of the cost of what it is buying, and advertising is one of its more expensive purchases.

Industry will force advertising to change, because it will want the cost of advertising to be cheaper; it will also want to see more clearly what it is getting for its money. For it is inconceivable that while the rest of the business world is increasing its efficiency and its profitability advertising can, by some unknown dispensation, remain immutable. Advertising must become more efficient and more profitable too, and it is palpably not becoming so at present. Its whole structure inhibits efficiency, and its profitability goes steadily down. It will have to recognise the warning signs.

Imagine yourself to be the marketing director of a major company in twenty years' time. How might you set about the task of planning your next advertising campaign?

You may or you may not be satisfied with the campaign just ended or still running: let us assume you are not – it adds force to the example, because in the future you will have no need to think three months ahead if you want to change your agency.

There will be little in your marketing department that differs from today, except that there will probably be more electronic equipment in the office, and possibly a team of media analysts to plan the deployment of your budget. Basically, your staff will still be organised into product groups, each of them responsible to you for some part of your company's range.

Your first decision will be to agree a budget. Your product manager will recommend a figure, based on the objectives he has set; you will assess this in the context of total product range requirements and eventually agree a sum. At the same time, your product manager will have produced a document which sets out the strategic objectives of the campaign under the separate headings of marketing, advertising, creative, media and promotional targets (the last four being detailed elements of the first); note that he is taking his planning far further than he does today – the definition of advertising objectives is at present very much an agency function.

This document will in effect be a brief for those who will produce the campaign, and after you have approved it your product manager will proceed with the business of setting these people to work. Depending on the degree of autonomy you allow him, you may or may not assist him. Let us assume you do, so that we can see what happens.

Your budget has been fixed at £1,000,000 (today it would be half that amount, but we must allow for inflation). Of this you have decided to set aside £350,000 for sales promotion activities, leaving £650,000 for above-the-line (media advertising) expenditure.

Your immediate priority will be the selection of creative services (there are still a few old-fashioned 'agencies' in operation, but they are little used and possess only mediocre creative talent). You have been using the same creative service for the last two years, but you are not completely happy since you feel that much more could be made of the creative opportunities on your account. You therefore decide to discuss your problem with another creative unit, which has been well spoken of by one of your friends and the advertisements from which, for other products, you have seen and admired. You tell your present consultant that you are delaying a decision on whether or not to ask him to produce work for your new campaign until you have discussed the problem elsewhere.

You are impressed when you meet the new creative unit. They quickly show an intelligent appreciation of the situation and make observations which indicate a positive and imaginative creative approach. There is, however, a snag: when you ask them what sort of fee they would require for their services they quote a figure of £30,000, which is twice what you have been paying before. Although this sum would cover all creative work, the supervision of production and schedule rotation, you are reluctant to agree to it. You therefore tell them that you feel it to be on the high side and that you will go away and think it over. They are quite happy for you to do this, but they suggest that you will find it difficult to obtain work of that quality for less.

On your return to your office you discuss the situation with your product manager, who is very enthusiastic and feels the fee is reasonable, and also with your managing director, who is a cautious individual and advises you to shop around before coming to a decision. You think that this is a reasonable suggestion and you act on it.

In the course of the next few days you visit two other creative units. Neither of them displays the same level of creative competence as the first; indeed, one of them is no better than your present consultants, but would cost more, and the other asks the same price (£30,000) as the one by whom you were so impressed but for work which you believe will be of lower quality.

After further discussion at the office, you therefore make your final decision: you accept the £30,000 fee and instruct the first consultancy to begin work on its creative proposals. At the same time you inform your old suppliers that you will not be using their services for the new campaign.

The new people quickly submit their recommendations. Your product manager shares your approval of them, but suggests a number of points which need to be validated through advertising research before the proposals can be taken further. He calls in a research company and briefs them to do this. The results fully confirm that the campaign is based on a valid concept and that the creative implementation of it successfully communicates a positive selling proposition.

The time has now come for you to take two further steps: you must brief your media broker[1] and you must discuss promotional plans with your promotions agency.

You outline to your media broker the creative constraints of the campaign, the media objectives in terms of prime and secondary audience targets, the size of the budget available, and the broad media strategy worked out by your own analysts. On thc last point, you indicate that there will be a total of £620,000 for media expenditure, including your broker's fee; this is the original £650,000 less £30,000 which your creative consultants need for production. Your media broker works on the basis of rebating to you all commissions he receives from booked space and air-time (15 per cent) and charging you a fee; on the budget you have given him, therefore, he will rebate to you £73,000 (15 per cent of £630,000, less his fee of £10,000).[2] There are, incidentally, rumours in the media world about this time that the press, television, radio, cinema and outdoor contractors are seriously considering the total abolition of the now anachronistic commission arrangement, since such discounts are inevitably rebated to clients by brokers; this step would involve a restructuring of all advertising rates.

A programme of sales promotion activity, based on the budget of £350,000 (including the agency's fee), is agreed; this is planned as an intrinsic part of the total campaign both in timing and character. Your product manager will be responsible for the co-ordination of all this activity, although its detailed implementation and control will be in the hands of the promotions agency.

By this time, work is well advanced on the production of the advertisements themselves, and final testing, if necessary, can be carried out. Your campaign is soon ready to start.

We can now compare the total cost of this programme with what would happen in today's conditions. It is important to remember that we are comparing like with like, for nothing that happens today will not happen in twenty years' time; all that will change will be the procedure by which similar objectives are achieved. First of all, we shall examine the cost comparison in tabular form, after which we can identify the detail of the redistribution of effort and responsibility in the two operations:

[1] Alternatively, if you do not employ one, you must plan and buy your own campaign.
[2] He will also be under no illusions about the need for efficient work; he will know that your analysts will check the quality of his buying exhaustively.

Old Method		*New Method*	
Budget	£1,000,000	Budget	£1,000,000
Media advertising	£650,000	Media advertising	£650,000
Promotion	£350,000	Promotion	£350,000
Media expenditure	£620,000	Media expenditure	£620,000
Production	£30,000	Creative fee	£30,000
Promotion	£350,000	Production	£30,000
		Media fee	£10,000
		Promotion	£350,000
			£1,040,000
		Less media rebate	£83,000
Total expenditure	£1,000,000	Total expenditure	£957,000

Note: any other form of expenditure, such as research, print, etc., will be common to both calculations.

The difference in cost to the client is shown by these figures to be £43,000 in favour of the new method. This sum can either be saved and put to some other purpose, or it can be added to the budget to buy more space or air-time. Either way, the new procedure is almost 5 per cent more cost-effective than the old on the budget in question. This comparison will differ, of course, according to the size of the budget and the level of service fees, but the difference will almost always favour the new method, since fees will be lower than the commission on all but minimal advertising appropriations.

The interesting point emerging from the comparison is that all parties involved are well paid for their labours under the new arrangement, yet the total amount handed over by the client is £43,000 less than if he uses a traditional agency; what is more, the agency of today is lucky if it makes 2 per cent profit on turnover, which is a significant indication of the burden of overheads it carries.

Under the new system the two main participants in the operation – the creative consultancy and the media broker – will consist of relatively small staffs, being the equivalent of agency creative and media departments. A creative unit can perform its function perfectly well with a few people: an 'ideas' man to formulate the basic concept, a copywriter to fill in the details of copy and a layout artist or visualiser to translate the visual idea into some definable form. In addition, there must be a typographer and/or a production executive who can supervise the transition from layout through artwork to the printed proof. In all, a maximum of four or five people is enough to see a press campaign through from first thoughts to finished advertisement (there will be at least two more people for television campaigns); add secretaries, accountants and the usual services, and allow for several campaigns a year, and we finish up with about ten people working on accounts worth perhaps £200,000 a year in fee values (the equivalent of an agency billing of £1·3 million, which would require a staff of about sixty).

The same is true of media, only more so. One man can plan a media schedule; another can buy it. Several plans can be produced by the same person: several can be bought. Thus the economics of running such a service are very favourable. A small partnership of four people, for example, with a supporting staff of, say, three could comfortably handle media billings of £5 million a year, bringing in fees of anything up to £100,000. An agency with a turnover of this size would need a staff of approximately 100–120.

How, therefore, can we account for the fact that this new method of controlling the advertising function will involve so few people, compared with the present system? There are two major factors which contribute to the possibility. Firstly, clients themselves will assume responsibility for far more of the initial planning operation than they do at the moment. Indeed, the product manager could be said to have taken over almost entirely the role of account executive, since it will be largely through him that the process will be co-ordinated and controlled. It has already been shown how his own plan will have much wider terms of reference than it has at present, including as it does the formulation of advertising goals and the specification of the broad areas of strategic advertising actitity. Thus the duplication of effort represented by client service departments in today's agencies will be removed and the anomalous situation rationalised. Account groups are a significant and costly proportion of an agency's payroll, being on average 20 per cent of staff and possibly 30 per cent of salaries.

The second factor is that under the new system there will be no place for an agency marketing or research department. Clients will be totally responsible for their own marketing operations. The situation which now exists, whereby the function of agency marketing departments is severely limited and often superfluous, will change dramatically, and this further duplication of activity will come to an end.

Thus the transition from old to new will mean that only the really specialist functional areas of advertising will remain outside the direct control of the client, a situation which will give the lie to the jealous professionalism of today's agencies. It is questionable whether more than a handful of agency people have appreciated the direction of the trend, or indeed whether advertising men have even looked twenty years ahead. This perhaps is why the industry is so extraordinarily complacent: it can imagine no alternative to the methods and structures of today; it lives for the present because its past has had a continuous sameness about it which seems to indicate a similar future. In classical Greece the tragedians would have recognised this as *hybris*, the pride before the fall.

Of course, as time goes on, the truth of the situation will become easier to comprehend, but harder for advertising to accept since things will have gone too far. Even now, some of the ablest creative people are freelance consultants, and every day that passes will see these consultancies grow stronger and the agencies weaker; exactly when the balance will tip from one side to the other is impossible to predict, but, the moment it does, advertising as it is known today will die.

Creativity, media expertise, research services, sales promotion – all these will fragment into their specialist areas; marketing, control, direction, co-ordination – these will be the prerogatives of the client, who will be the final instigator and arbiter of advertising strategy as it really is, an inherent and integral part of marketing planning, not a separate state of the realm. The client will of right be king; he *should* know his business better than anyone else. He has for far too long suffered the indignity of being told by others that he is wrong. Why? Because for far too long he has had no reason for saying that he knows better. Now at last he has equipped himself more fully, more efficiently and more economically to run his business as only he knows it should be run.[1]

We have therefore argued the case as follows: the agency will disappear and the consultancy will become the accepted thing; this will

[1] See Fig. 8 for a diagrammatical comparison between the present and suggested future operational structures of the advertising industry. For a more detailed version of the present structure, see Fig. 2 (p. 52).

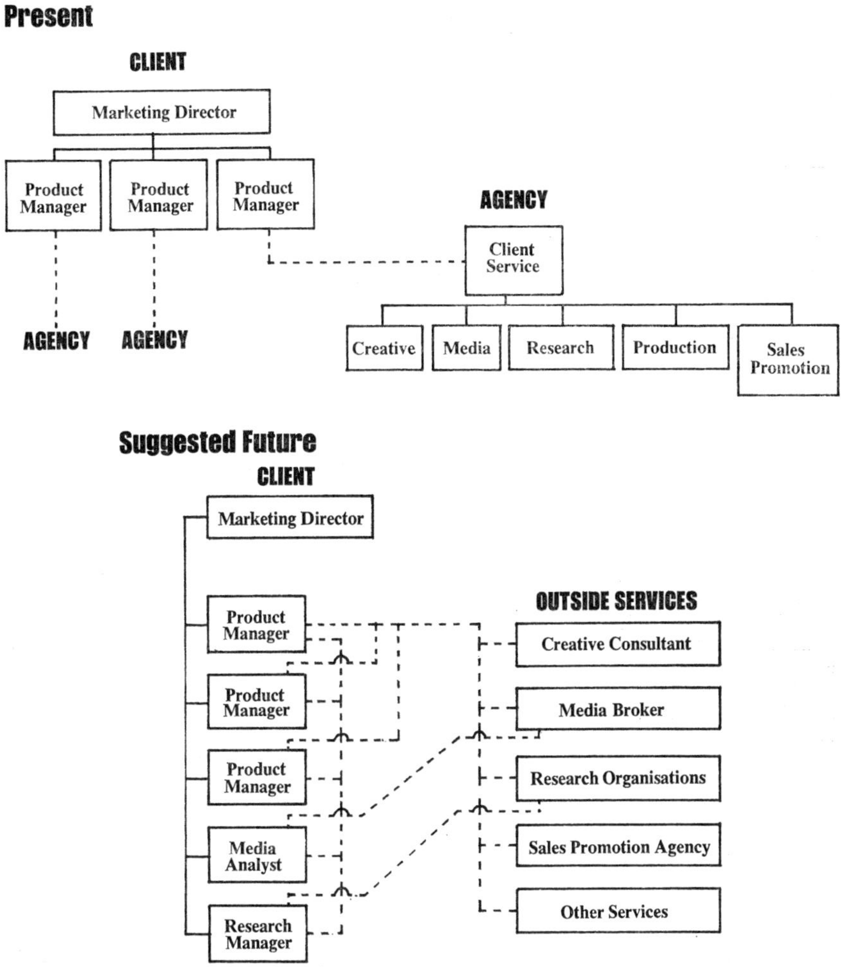

Fig. 8 Comparison between present and suggested future operational structures of advertising

happen because both the advertising industry and its clients want it so; and business will be the better for it.

But what of the ethics of advertising? What will come of all the nice, comfortable rules and regulations so carefully imposed by the IPA, whereby an agency is protected and cosseted from the assaults of its enemies? How will the new arrangement cope with the problems of competitive poachings, and accounts which have conflicting interests?

The situation today is a very cosy one, cultivated and preserved under the maternal supervision of the Institute, an anaesthetic which numbs any and all of its member agencies. Under its ruling, no member may 'solicit' business from another member, and no member may accept an account which can conceivably compete with business which that member already holds (this latter ruling is currently generously interpreted by the agencies but, quite naturally, rigorously observed by clients; frozen peas, for example, compete not only with canned or dried peas, but also with frozen fish fingers under another brand name). One should, of course, mention that some present-day agencies do not belong to the IPA and are therefore not subject to these somewhat inhibiting strictures.

The answer lies in the attitudes of industry itself. No company wants to surrender its secrets unthinkingly to its competitors; no company willingly exposes itself to retaliation; no company, in its right mind, is going to make itself vulnerable by omitting to consider the consequences of placing its business in the hands of suppliers who are also party to the confidences of other firms in the same market.

In other words, it is not the IPA which at the moment protects clients from breaches of confidence: it is the clients who protect themselves, because they are far too sensible of the consequences to do anything quite so stupid as to entrust their accounts to an agency which handles the business of one of their competitors. Of all the arguments which have arisen in recent years about conflicting accounts, I can think of none that have originated from the IPA – and certainly none that have stemmed from the agency: all have been the result of objections from existing clients to their agency's desire to take on what they regard as conflicting business. Clients are likely to be far more insistent in their interpretation of the rule than the IPA itself.

As for soliciting, what can be said? We have already seen how agencies disregard this rule. The line of demarcation between permitted promotion and downright poaching is not easy to trace; and in any case how does the IPA discover the tenor of that quiet conversation on the golf course or at the domestic dinner table, or even that such a conversation has taken place at all? The fact of the matter is that no agency today is protected from solicitation for its clients' business, whether a member of the IPA or not; the IPA's protection is protection in name only.

Surely the existence of such a rule is yet another example of the basic insecurity and lack of confidence on the part of the advertising business? Why should it need to be protected in this way? Are not the mutual trust and respect which are engendered by efficiency and good service the best protection an agency can have against the possibility of losing accounts? If a client is disposed to change his agency, he will do so in any event, solicited or not. The industry is far too much concerned with its professional etiquette, and far too little interested in the hard graft of developing and maintaining firm and durable relationships through the proper observance of its required obligations.

The future, therefore, presents no problems for those who understand the present. There is nothing, in the somewhat artificial and contrived atmosphere of today's activity, which can inhibit healthy and progressive development. Logically, the trend towards the refinement of advertising skills into the specific benefits of creative expertise and the provision of a service which is, and is seen to be, in demand, can only increase the need to stimulate business agreements based on the recognition of satisfactory performance. Unless advertising (whether in its present form or as it will be in years to come) accepts this as inevitable, it cannot prosper.

Thus the consultancies and 'ideas centres' which are now starting to come into being will have no use for the regulations imposed by the IPA. The IPA will, in time, disappear in its present form because its usefulness will rapidly evaporate; it can offer nothing of any lasting value to the emergent vitality of the business. And it will disappear because it will have nobody of any consequence or influence to represent. The new generation of advertising men will succeed not through protection but through their own ability and their own relevance to the needs of industry.

These new advertising organisations will prosper on the age-old principles of healthy competition and business efficiency, just as any other service industry must do. If I am dissatisfied with the service I obtain from my printer, I choose a new printer; if I do not get what I want from the firm which supplies the oil to feed my boilers, I buy from somewhere else; if my company cannot obtain satisfactory secretaries from one appointments bureau, I can select another; and so with my advertising.

Similarly, whether I change my supplier as a result of my own dissatisfaction or because of an approach by a new supplier who convinces me that his price, service or quality is better, it is all the same: it remains my inalienable right to do so. Advertising spends its entire time attempting to switch customers from one brand loyalty to another; why therefore should it object if the same principles and practices are used for its own product? Under the present system, it seems that whereas clients have a right to be informed and persuaded of the qualities of all other products and services which they may need, their advertising is sacrosanct; and this is patently absurd.

In the future, this anomaly will no longer apply. Advertising will be a service on the same basis as any other. There will be no need for IPA protection, because the conditions and attitudes which made such protection necessary or desirable will have disappered. All advertising companies – creative units, media brokers, merchandising specialists, marketing and research consultants – will have the freedom and the incentive to look for new business wherever it can be found and wherever they can show that they have a better product to offer. They will be competing in a free and open market, where the best will be successful and prices will match demand.

It is difficult to see how anyone can maintain that such a situation is not an improvement on the present arrangement – anyone, that is, except the diehard and conservative traditionalists who populate the advertising agencies of today. One is led almost to feel that industry regards advertising as something of a curiosity, which is in a strange way immune from the forces which change and influence the modern world, but the illusion is quickly dispelled: while companies may have tolerated this less than perfect phenomenon for a very long time, and in so doing may have given the impression that they are well satisfied, they must nevertheless soon display their disenchantment. They will both prompt changes in advertising and accept the change it brings upon itself.

This is really the central point of the whole argument. It is the changing standards of business efficiency which will ultimately force the rationalisation in advertising to take place. For a few years after the Second World War advertising developed its skills and techniques more rapidly than at any other time in its history; during this same period industry on the whole changed very little, particularly in Britain where the ravages of war had not, ironically, provided the opportunity to start again with new attitudes, new plant and new methods. Advertising after the war inherited nothing except the chance to improve, and it grasped this chance with outstretched hands, reaching in the process a degree of refinement which the rest of industry was not destined to achieve for another decade. Since then it has stood still, and its clients have gradually caught and outstripped it; they are now waiting for it to match their own progress.

The 1970s therefore will be the watershed in advertising's growth. By 1980 the trend towards specialist companies and the fragmentation of activity, coupled with the re-emergence of a much more complete 'advertising man' and the transfer of authority and decision into the hands of the client, will be well advanced. The lead in this direction will continue, as now, to be given by the best people in today's agencies; the result will be that, as more and more able advertising men – the top creative thinkers in particular – realise the opportunities which exist outside the agencies' cloistered isolation, and take advantage of them, the quality of the agencies themselves will fall, until at last they will disappear, atrophied through lack of use and an insufficiency of clients.

Whatever the agencies themselves may say, advertising is still very much an art; true, the art is practised with the aid of some fairly scientific techniques, but it remains essentially an art and not a science. What makes it an art is its central creative function, the most important part of the whole and the criterion upon which, and only which, it must be judged. Without creative ability an agency which can provide the best service in any other area is a broken reed. Creative excellence is the quality sought above all others by any client. Accounts change hands for creative reasons more often than any other. And perhaps most important of all, creative work is *seen*; it is the living evidence of an agency's ability, obvious to all – clients, public and other agencies alike.

Within the formal structure of the agency, creative people often find their artistic style cramped. They also often find themselves forced to undertake administrative duties for which they are unsuited and which they dislike intensely. Little wonder, therefore, that they should play the lead in this new act of the advertising drama by recognising both the necessity and the profit of an independent function, where their own attitudes are given full scope to blossom and develop, where they can talk direct to clients in their own language, explaining and defending their own ideas, and where they must, and do, accept total responsibility for the campaigns they write.

It is, as has been said, the best creative people who have made this move. There are still good creative people in the agencies, but they are dwindling and will become even fewer. The reason for good staff moving out and indifferent staff remaining behind is largely the greater confidence which better people have in their own ability, which reacts unfavourably to the inhibiting constraints of agency organisation. Through this confidence they can succeed in their new environment and produce creative advertising of a high standard which they are able to present competently to their clients.

What effect these changes will have on advertisements themselves – the written and spoken word, the images which face us on the page, screen or hoarding – it is virtually impossible to say. The chances are that they will improve, in two ways: their aesthetic quality should be higher and their effectiveness strònger, if for no other reason than that they will not have been emasculated by a committee. The client/creator interface should by definition provide a better brief and a better campaign consonant with the character of the company for which it is produced.

Certainly there is no reason to suppose that the quality of advertising will be lowered by the new developments in the business. All the conditions will be right for the production of advertisements which are not only better but cheaper, due entirely to the more economic employment of skills and the centralisation of the control function into the hands of the client. This is the most important change in organised advertising that will, if we have read the signs correctly, take place over the next few years.

All this must inevitably be a bleak prospect for most advertising people. They will dispute the forecast hotly because it amounts to the destruction of all that they hold most dear. Yet, if they do, they are once more showing clearly the attitudes which have caused the present mismatch of advertising's services to industry; it is precisely because there has been no willingness to change, indeed even to recognise the necessity for change, that advertising has so patently failed to equip itself adequately to meet the demands, obvious or latent, which may be placed upon it.

The research which has from time to time been commissioned to discover what industry wants from advertising has invariably begged a vitally important question: every survey has assumed that, whatever industry's requirements may be, they can be satisfied by the advertising agency; no other possibility has been allowed. Had such research (in the manner of most professional marketing enquiries) started by identifying industry's needs so that appropriate satisfactions of those needs could be supplied, the results might have been very different. As it is, the information provided by these investigations is of little use, except possibly as a means of agency comfort, because the questions which were asked so clearly avoided the central issues.

The fact is, however, that no matter how strongly advertising people may argue that our prognosis is mistaken, and that the future will be very different from the one we have postulated, it is the best of them who have already begun to make our forecast a reality and to ensure the future lifeblood of the industry. Some of the best work in British advertising is now being produced by the consultancies and workshops we have identified as the basis of the business in years to come. These consultancies represent an emergent evolutionary process, the embryo of a new animal better suited to his environment, better able to function effectively, better equipped to defend himself.

A new chapter has been begun in the annals of British advertising, but no more than its opening lines has been written. Its authors are the men and women of the industry who as yet see its schematic development dimly. Some will have a brighter vision than the rest, and the story will unfold. *Vis omnia vincit?*

Index